INTERPRETATIONS

Vol 7

JOJI LOCATELLI AND VEERA VÄLIMÄKI

*Photographs by Jonna Jolkin
and Charly Barros
Illustrations by Laura Bazzalo*

POM POM PRESS
LONDON

Published in 2020 by Pom Pom Press
Text © 2020 Joji Locatelli & Veera Välimäki
Photographs © 2020 Jonna Jolkin & Charly Barros
Illustrations: Laura Bazzalo
www.interpretationsbyjojiandveera.com

ISBN: 978-1-9160295-4-5
A catalogue record for this book is available from
the British Library.

Editors: Meghan Fernandes & Lydia Gluck
Managing Editor: Amy Collins
Publisher + Marketing Director: Belinda Johnson
UK Wholesale Manager + Community Liaison:
Sophie Heathscott
Features Editor: Francesca Baldry
Production Assistant + Retail Manager: Alice
Sleight
Social Media + Digital Content Coordinator:
Sofia Aatkar
Studio Managers: Iesha Parker +
Gayle Taliaferro Gilner

Printed in the UK by Pureprint Group Limited

POM POM PRESS
Hackney Downs Studios,
Charcoal Hall
Amhurst Terrace
London E8 2BT
United Kingdom
pompommag.com

CONTENTS

FOREWORD

We bring *Interpretations Volume 7* to life in 2020, a year in which a pandemic took the whole world by surprise and turned everything upside down.

As we get ready to write the foreword for a book that reads '*Volume 7*' on its cover, we wonder: can this really be considered just 'another volume'? Can anything created, edited, or added as part of a series this year really be considered just 'another piece'?

This is a book of knitting patterns, however, in order for it to be published, all working patterns had to be broken, all systems had to be updated. The book we present you is something totally new, unexpected, unplanned...

We always said that *Interpretations* would walk with us through life, through happiness and hardship. And here we are, publishing under extraordinary circumstances, but stronger than ever. It's almost as if reality is teasing us and laughing... at us? With us? Doesn't it make sense that such a different volume is a logical follow up to everything we've published before? It would be hard to imagine a truer record of reality.

This pattern collection was born at the end of 2019. We proposed the theme words: Root, Light, Wonder, Beyond, Natural, and Wild. We outlined the color palette and patterns and we planned a photoshoot together. We haven't seen each other in a very long time. It's actually the longest we've been apart.

We were going to reunite in the UK and photograph these designs in August, but early on we knew it would not be possible to travel and meet. Should we go ahead with the book? How to do it? The very reason we work on these books is to get together. To bring our two distant worlds to the same time and space. Did it make sense to write this book if we wouldn't be together at all?

It makes sense, total sense. We think this volume is a record of this year's events, and of the sorrow of being apart. We worked harder than ever (and perhaps more together than ever) and we made it happen.

We always carefully plan our photography. We pick a location, a wardrobe, we hire a photographer. We often get help to have our hair and make up done. None of that was possible for this volume because of lockdown, curfews, and social distancing rules, so we created a virtual scenario for us to work together.

Our photoshoots took place on the same day, at the same time, on opposite corners of the world. We planned to take photographs with similar angles and points of view that would look uniform, even when shot by different people. All the patterns were photographed within the boundaries of our homes: Veera's in Finland and Joji's in Argentina. This way we could translate the restrictions we had in our movements to our pattern photography too.

We edited these photos together to give them a sense of unity. We stayed in touch with each other during these sessions, trying to keep the feeling of togetherness we always bring to our books.

We believe this book is a success, and we are prouder than ever to present it to you, with all the challenges we faced to do it. Here's another Interpretations book of patterns to inspire you.

Joji and Veera

WONDER

I wake up in my warm bed. I wonder what day it is... then I wonder if it makes a difference. I think I've lost track of time. I've been living this dream so vividly for the past few months. Has it been years?

Living in repeat day after day, always following the same routine. I roll around and my partner is there. I see his chest moving up and down, breathing in a peaceful cadence. He's so calm. I wish I could feel that calmness in my own chest.

I put on woolen socks, walk half asleep to the kitchen and start my morning brew. Always the same roast, always the same smell that make my home feel warm. I walk back to bed and start working on this day's tasks. Always the same tasks. There are no surprises. I get easily bored, but in this dream, my home and the routine of work feel like blessings. What would I be doing if I didn't have this routine? What would I do if I didn't have the whole world waiting for me to act my role in this play?

It's a time of *uncertainty*. I used to be the one looking ahead, always planning, organizing and moving forward. But my dream has stopped in this day and the most challenging task seems to be living this today, over and over again.

At the end of this day, just another day, I sit back on the same chair, I grab my knitting and instinctively I make stitches. One after the other. Always the same movements, always the same combination, and always part of something bigger. At the end of every day I realize how small I am and how little control I actually have over things, even though I am a planner and an organizer. It is humbling and exciting to know how surprised we can all still be. How our story is not written in full.

If there were an author in this play, there are so many things I would ask them. Where is the plot going? What will happen next? But this author doesn't know the outcome, for it hasn't been thought out yet. We still have so much to discover. I sigh in relief. What a wonderful day tomorrow will be.

Oh what a wonder.

WONDER

BLURRY COWL

EVERGREEN CARDIGAN

BLURRY COWL

by Joji Locatelli

Born during a night of boredom, and of the desire to just feel the rhythm of the stitches in my hands, this cowl is both easy to make and easy to wear.

It's designed to resemble a triangular shawl wrapped around your neck... but it's not. Just slip it over your head and you are ready to go.

Designed for 2 skeins of DK-weight yarn, the cowl is worked from the top down. It features a blurry chevron texture on top, stripes in the middle, and a lacy ribbing near the edge.

BLURRY COWL

SIZES

ONE SIZE.

Finished measurements: 22¼" [56 cm] in circumference and 21½" [53.5 cm] long (after blocking). See schematics below.

MATERIALS

Yarn: 2 skeins of Merino DK by Wobble Gobble Yarn (100% Merino; 231 yds [211 m] / 100 g). 1 skein in Color 1 (sample shown in colorway Dogwood), or approx. 231 yds [211 m] of DK weight yarn; and 1 skein in Color 2 (sample shown in colorway Rust), or approx. 231 yds [211 m] of DK weight yarn.

Needles: US 6 [4 mm] needles, 24" long.

Other: Stitch markers and tapestry needle.

GAUGE

19 sts and 30 rows = 4" [10 cm] on US 6 [4 mm] needles in Stockinette stitch. *Before you measure, please take the time to wash and block your swatch in the same manner that you will wash and block your cowl.*

FINISHED MEASUREMENTS

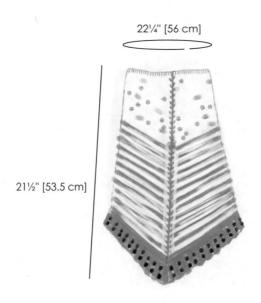

22¼" [56 cm]

21½" [53.5 cm]

BLURRY COWL

DIRECTIONS

BEGINNING

With Color 1, CO 3 sts. Knit 6 rows.

Next row (RS): K3, pick up and knit 3 sts along the side of your little rectangle (1 st from every purl ridge). Pick up and knit 3 stitches from the CO edge. *You should have 9 sts.*

From now on, always slip the 1st st of each row knitwise.

Set-up row (WS): Sl1, k to end.

Row 1 (RS): Sl1, k2, pm, m1R, k1, m1L, pm, k1, pm, m1R, k1, m1L, pm, k3. *You should have 13 sts.*

Row 2 (WS): Sl1, k2, sm, p to last m, sm, k3.

Row 3: Sl1, k2, sm, m1R, k to m, m1L, sm, k1, sm, m1R, k to m, m1L, sm, k3. *You should have 17 sts.*

Row 4: Sl1, k2, sm, p to last m, sm, k3.

Repeat **Rows 3-4** twice more. *You should have 25 sts.*

CHEVRONS SECTION

Row 1: Sl1, k2, sm, m1R, p1, (k7, p1) to m, m1L, sm, k1, sm, m1R, p1, (k7, p1) to m, m1L, sm, k3. *29 sts.*

Row 2: Sl1, k2, sm, k3, (p5, k3) to m, sm, p1, sm, k3, (p5, k3) to m, sm, k3.

Row 3: Sl1, k2, sm, m1R, p3, (k5, p3) to m, m1L, sm, k1, sm, m1R, p3, (k5, p3) to m, m1L, sm, k3. *33 sts.*

Row 4: Sl1, k2, sm, k5, (p3, k5) to m, sm, p1, sm, k5, (p3, k5) to m, sm, k3.

Row 5: Sl1, k2, sm, m1R, p5, (k3, p5) to m, m1L, sm, k1, sm, m1R, p5, (k3, p5) to m, m1L, sm, k3. *37 sts.*

Row 6: Sl1, k2, sm, k7, (p1, k7) to m, sm, p1,

sm, k7, (p1, k7) to m, sm, k3.

Row 7: Sl1, k2, sm, m1R, p7, (k1, p7) to m, m1L, sm, k1, sm, m1R, p7, (k1, p7) to m, m1L, sm, k3. *41 sts.*

Row 8: Sl1, k2, sm, k4, (p1, k7) to 5 sts from m, p1, k4, sm, p1, sm, k4, (p1, k7) to 5 sts from m, p1, k4, sm, k3.

Row 9: Sl1, k2, sm, m1R, p4, (k1, p7) to 5 sts from m, k1, p4, m1L, sm, k1, sm, m1R, p4, (k1, p7) to 5 sts from m, k1, p4, m1L, sm, k3. *45 sts.*

Row 10: Sl1, k2, sm, k4, (p3, k5) to 7 sts from m, p3, k4, sm, p1, sm, k4, (p3, k5) to 7 sts from m, p3, k4, sm, k3.

Row 11: Sl1, k2, sm, m1R, p4, (k3, p5) to 7 sts from m, k3, p4, m1L, sm, k1, sm, m1R, p4, (k3, p5) to 7 sts from m, k3, p4, m1L, sm, k3. *49 sts.*

Row 12: Sl1, k2, sm, p1, (k3, p5) to 4 sts from m, k3, p1, sm, p1, sm, p1, (k3, p5) to 4 sts from m, k3, p1, sm, k3.

Row 13: Sl1, k2, sm, m1R, k1, (p3, k5) to 4 sts from m, p3, k1, m1L, sm, k1, sm, m1R, k1, (p3, k5) to 4 sts from m, p3, k1, m1L, sm, k3. *53 sts.*

Row 14: Sl1, k2, sm, p3, (k1, p7) to 4 sts from m, k1, p3, sm, p1, sm, p3, (k1, p7) to 4 sts from m, k1, p3, sm, k3.

Row 15: Sl1, k2, sm, m1R, k3, (p1, k7) to 4 sts from m, p1, k3, m1L, sm, k1, sm, m1R, k3, (p1, k7) to 4 sts from m, p1, k3, m1L, sm, k3. *57 sts.*

Row 16: Sl1, k2, sm, k1, (p7, k1) to m, sm, p1, sm, k1, (p7, k1) to m, sm, k3.

Work **Rows 1-16** twice more. *You should have 121 sts.*

STRIPED SECTION

Row 1 (RS): Sl1, k2, sm, m1R, k to m, m1L, sm, k1, sm, m1R, k to m, m1L, sm, k3.

Row 2 (WS): Sl1, k2, sm, p to last marker, sm, k3.

Change to Color 2 and work **Rows 1-2**. Then change to Color 1 and work **Rows 1-2** once more. *You should have 133 sts.*

Row 7: Change to Color 2. K3, remove m, k to m, m1L, sm, k1, sm, m1R, k to m, remove

15

m, k3, join for working in the round. Place marker.

Round 8: K to end of round. *You should have 135 sts.*

WORK IN THE ROUND

Round 1: Change to Color 1, k1, ssk, k to m, m1L, sm, k1, sm, m1R, k to 3 sts from m, k2tog, k1.

Rounds 2, 4, 6, 8: K to end of round.

Round 3: Change to Color 2, k1, ssk, k to m, m1L, sm, k1, sm, m1R, k to 3 sts from m, k2tog, k1.

Round 5: Change to Color 1, k1, ssk, k to m, m1L, sm, k1, sm, m1R, k to 3 sts from m, k2tog, k1.

Round 7: Change to Color 2, k to m, m1L, sm, k1, sm, m1R, k end. 137 sts.

Repeat **Rounds 1-8** 4 more times. *2 sts will be increased after each repeat. You should have 145 sts.*

Break yarn Color 1.

BOTTOM BORDER

Round 1: With Color 2. K1, ssk, k1, (p1, ktbl, p1, k1) to m, m1L, sm, k1, sm, m1R, (k1, p1, ktbl, p1) to 4 sts from m, k1, k2tog, k1.

Round 2: K2, (p2, ktbl, p1) to 2 sts from m, p2, sm, k1, sm, p2, (p1, ktbl, p2) to 2 sts from m, k2.

Round 3: K1, ssk, (p1, ktbl, p1, k1) to 1 st from m, p1, m1L, sm, k1, sm, m1R, p1, (k1, p1, ktbk, p1) to 3 sts from m, k2tog, k1.

Round 4: K2, (k3, p1) to 2 sts from m, k2, sm, k1, sm, k2, (p1, k3) to 2 sts from end, k2.

Round 5: K1, ssk, k2tog, yo, k1, (yo, s2kp, yo, k1) to 2 sts from m, yo, ssk, m1L, sm, k1, sm, m1R, k2tog, yo, (k1, yo, s2kp, yo) to 6 sts from m, k1, yo, ssk, k2tog, k1.

Round 6: K4, p1, (k3, p1) to 3 sts from m, k3, sm, k1, sm, k3, (p1, k3) to 5 sts from end, p1, k4.

Round 7: K2, ktbl, p1, k1, (p1, ktbl, p1, k1) to 3 sts from m, p1, ktbl, p1, m1L, sm, k1, sm, m1R, p1, ktbl, p1, (k1, p1, ktbl, p1) to 5 sts from end, k1, p1, ktbl, k2.

Round 8: K2, ktbl, p2, (p1, ktbl, p2) to m, sm, k1, sm, (p2, ktbl, p1) to 5 sts from end, p2, ktbl, k2.

Round 9: K1, ssk, p1, k1, (p1, ktbl, p1, k1) to m, m1L, sm, k1, sm, m1R, (k1, p1, ktbk, p1) to 5 sts from m, k1, p1, k2tog, k1.

Round 10: (K3, p1) to 1 st from m, k1, sm, k1, sm, k1, (p1, k3) to end.

Round 11: K1, ssk, k1, (yo, s2kp, yo, k1) to 1 st from m, k1, m1L, sm, k1, sm, m1R, k1, (k1, yo, s2kp, yo) to 4 sts from end, k1, k2tog, k1.

Round 12: K2, p1, (k3, p1) to 2 sts from m, k2, sm, k1, sm, k2, (p1, k3) to 3 sts from m, p1, k2.

Round 13: K1, ssk, (p1, ktbl, p1, k1) to 2 sts from m, p1, ktbl, m1L, sm, k1, sm, m1R, ktbl, p1, (k1, p1, ktbl, p1) to 3 sts from end, k2tog, k1.

Round 14: K2, (p1, ktbl) to 1 st from m, p1, sm, k1, sm, p1, (ktbl, p1) to 2 sts from end, k2.

Round 15: K2, (p1, ktbl) to 1 st from m, p1, m1L, sm, k1, sm, m1R, p1, (ktbl, p1) to 2 sts from end, k2.

Round 16: K2, (p1, ktbl) to m, sm, k1, sm, (ktbl, p1) to 2 sts from end, k2.

Round 17: K1, ssk, ktbl, (p1, ktbl) to m, m1L, sm, k1, sm, m1R, (ktbl, p1) to 3 sts from end, k2tog, k1.

Round 18: BO all sts in pattern.

FINISHING

Weave in all yarn ends and block the cowl using your preferred method.

EVERGREEN CARDIGAN

by Veera Välimäki

The soft whisper of pines and spruces, the moss beneath my toes; it's the wonder of the forest, always the same yet always changing. The deep forest green color brings my thoughts to a fairytale world. These cables will always carry me to my happy place, that place of wonder where every twist brings me joy.

This cardigan is worked in one piece from the top down with minimal shaping. The cables make this a classic addition to your wardrobe, warm and lovely to wear from season to season.

EVERGREEN CARDIGAN

SIZES

1 (2, 3, 4, 5, 6, 7, 8, 9). Shown in size 3 on 38" bust.

Finished chest measurements: 36 (40, 44, 48, 52, 56, 60, 64, 68)" [90 (100, 110, 120, 130, 140, 150, 160, 170) cm] buttoned. Choose a size with approx. 4" [10 cm] of positive ease. See schematics below.

MATERIALS

Yarn: 5 (5, 6, 6, 7, 8, 8, 8, 9) skeins of Suoma DK by Kässäkerho Pom Pom (100% Finnsheep Wool (non-SW); 263 yds [240 m] / 100 g). Approx. 1180 (1310, 1440, 1570, 1720, 1840, 1970, 2120, 2250) yds [1080 (1200, 1320, 1440, 1570, 1680, 1790, 1900, 2060) m] of DK weight yarn. Sample shown in color Metsä (dark green).

Needles: US 7 [4.5 mm] and US 2½ [3 mm] circular needles, 32" [80 cm] long or longer, and dpns in each size for sleeves (if not using magic loop technique).

Other: Six ½" [1.5 cm] buttons, stitch markers, cable needle, tapestry needle, and blocking aids. Optional, but recommended: Row counter.

GAUGE

20 sts and 31 rows = 4" [10 cm] in cable pattern using larger needles. *Before you measure, please take the time to wash and block your swatch in the same manner that you will wash and block your cardigan.*

FINISHED MEASUREMENTS

8 (8¾, 9½, 10½, 11½, 12, 13½, 14¾, 15½)" [20 (22, 24, 27, 29, 32, 34, 37, 39) cm]

22½" [56 cm]

12 (13, 14, 15½, 17, 19, 20, 22, 23)" [30 (33, 36, 39, 43, 47, 50, 52, 55) cm]

14" [35 cm] all sizes

36 (40, 44, 48, 52, 56, 60, 64, 68)" [90 (100, 110, 120, 130, 140, 150, 160, 170) cm]

EVERGREEN CARDIGAN

CABLES USED

See all charts at the end of the pattern.

Cable A

Worked over 16 sts.

Row 1: C4F, knit 8, C4B.

Row 2 and all even rows: Purl.

Row 3: K2, C4F, k4, C4B, k2.

Row 5: K4, C4F, C4B, k4.

Repeat **Rows 1-6** for cable.

Cable B

Worked over 6 sts.

Row 1, 5 and 7: Knit.

Row 2 and all even rows: Purl.

Row 3: C6F.

Repeat **Rows 1-8** for cable.

Cable C

Worked over 6 sts.

Row 1, 5 and 7: Knit.

Row 2 and all even rows: Purl.

Row 3: C6B.

Repeat **Rows 1-8** for cable.

COLLAR

Using the smaller needle, CO 100 sts (all sizes). Do not join. Work 12 rows in garter st.

SHOULDER INCREASES

Change to larger needles and begin cable pattern, short row shaping and shoulder increases as follows.

Row 1 (RS): P2, k16 (for cable A), p1, k3, m1R, pm, p1, m1L, k3, p1, k16 (for cable A), p1, k12 (for cables B and C), p1, k16 (for cable A), p1, k3, m1R, p1, pm, m1L, k3, p1, k16 (for cable A), p2.

Row 2 (WS, short row): K2, p16, k1, p4, m1L (purl), sm, k1, m1R (purl), p4, k1, p16 (cable A), k1, p12 (cables C and B), k1, p16 (cable A), k1, p4, m1L (purl), k1, sm, m1R (purl), p4, k1, W&T.

Row 3 (RS, short row): P1, k5, m1R, sm, p1, m1L, k5, p1, [C4F, k8, C4B] (row 1 of cable A), p1, k12, p1, [C4F, k8, C4B] (row 1 of cable A), p1, k5, m1R, p1, sm, m1L, k5, p1, W&T.

Row 4 (WS, short row): K1, p6, m1L, sm, k1, m1R, p6, k1, p16, k1, p12, k1, p16, k1, p6, m1L, k1, sm, m1R, p6, k1, p2tog the wrap with the wrapped st, W&T.

Row 5 (RS, short row): K1, p1, [C6F] (row 3 of cable B), p1, m1R, sm, p1, m1L, p1, [C6B] (row 3 of cable C), p1, [k2, C4F, k4, C4B, k2] (row 3 of cable A), p1, [C6B, C6F] (row 3 of cables C and B), p1, [k2, C4F, k4, C4B, k2] (row 3 of cable A), p1, [C6F] (row 3 of cable B), p1, m1R, p1, sm, m1L, p1, [C6B] (row 3 of cable C), p1, k2tog the wrap with the wrapped st, W&T.

Row 6 (WS, short row): P1, k1, p6, k1, p1, m1L (purl), sm, k1, m1R (purl), p1, k1, p6, k1, p16, k1, p12, k1, p16, k1, p6, k1, p1, m1L (purl), k1, sm, m1R (purl), p1, k1, p6, k1, p1, p2tog the wrap with the wrapped st, W&T.

Row 7 (RS, short row): K2, p1, k6, p1, k2, m1R, sm, p1, m1L, k2, p1, k6, p1, [k4, C4F, C4B, k4] (row 5 of cable A), p1, k12, p1, [k4, C4F, C4B, k4] (row 5 of cable A), p1, k6, p1, k2, m1R, p1, sm, m1L, k2, p1, k6, p1, k1, k2tog the wrap with the wrapped st, W&T.

Row 8 (WS, short row): P2, k1, p6, k1, p3, m1L (purl), sm, k1, m1R (purl), p3, k1, p6, k1, p16, k1, p12, k1, p16, k1, p6, k1, p3, m1L (purl), k1, sm, m1R (purl), p3, k1, p6, k1, p2, p2tog the wrap with the wrapped st, W&T.

Row 9 (RS, short row): K3, p1, k6, p1, k4, m1R, sm, p1, m1L, k4, p1, k6, p1, [C4F, k8, C4B] (row 1 of cable A), p1, k12, p1, [C4F, k8, C4B] (row 1 of cable A), p1, k6, p1, k4, m1R, p1, sm, m1L, k4, p1, k6, p1, k2, k2tog the wrap with the wrapped st, W&T.

Row 10 (WS, short row): P3, k1, p6, k1, p5, m1L (purl), sm, k1, m1R (purl), p5, k1, p6, k1, p16, k1, p12, k1, p16, k1, p6, k1, p5, m1L (purl), k1, sm, m1R (purl), p5, k1, p6, k1, p3, p2tog the wrap with the wrapped st, p12, k2.

Short rows are now completed; continue with full rows as follows. Note: You will keep increasing 4 sts on every row, working a purled increase first following by 6 knitted increases to add more repeats of cables C and B.

Row 11 (RS): P2, [k2, C4F, k4, C4B, k2] (row 3 of cable A), [p1, k6] twice, m1R (purl), sm, p1, m1L (purl), [k6, p1] twice, [k2, C4F, k4, C4B, k2] (row 3 of cable A), p1, k12, p1, [k2, C4F, k4, C4B, k2] (row 3 of cable A), [p1, k6] twice, m1R (purl), p1, sm, m1L (purl), [k6, p1] twice, [k2, C4F, k4, C4B, k2] (row 3 of cable A, *Note: you need to pick up the last wrap at the same time as you work the C4F*), p2.

Row 12 (WS): K2, p16, k1, [p6, k1] twice, m1L (purl), sm, k1, m1R (purl), k1, [p6, k1] twice, p16, k1, p12, k1, p16, [k1, p6] twice, k1, m1L (purl), k1, sm, m1R (purl), [k1, p6] twice, k1, p16, k2.

Row 13: P2, [k4, C4F, C4B, k4] (row 5 of cable A), p1, [C6F (row 3 of cable B), p1] twice, k1, m1R, sm, p1, m1L, k1, [p1, C6B (row 3 of cable C)] twice, p1, [k4, C4F, C4B, k4] (row 5 of cable A), p1, [C6B, C6F] (row 3 of cables C and B), p1, [k4, C4F, C4B, k4] (row 5 of cable A), p1, [C6F (row 3 of cable B), p1] twice, k1, m1R, p1, sm, m1L, k1, [p1, C6B (row 3 of cable C)] twice, p1, [k4, C4F, C4B, k4] (row 5 of cable A), p2.

Row 14: K2, p16, k1, [p6, k1] twice, p2, m1L (purl), sm, k1, m1R (purl), p2, k1, [p6, k1] twice, p16, k1, p12, k1, p16, [k1, p6] twice, k1, p2, m1L (purl), k1, sm, m1R (purl), p2, [k1, p6] twice, k1, p16, k2.

Row 15: P2, [C4F, k8, C4B] (row 1 of cable A), p1, [k6, p1] twice, k3, m1R, sm, p1, m1L, k3, [p1, k6] twice, p1, [C4F, k8, C4B] (row 1 of cable A), p1, k12, p1, [C4F, k8, C4B] (row 1 of cable A), p1, [k6, p1] twice, k3, m1R, p1, sm, m1L, k3, [p1, k6] twice, p1,

[C4F, k8, C4B] (row 1 of cable A), p2.

Row 16: K2, p16, k1, [p6, k1] twice, p4, m1L (purl), sm, k1, m1R (purl), p4, k1, [p6, k1] twice, p16, k1, p12, k1, p16, [k1, p6] twice, k1, p4, m1L (purl), k1, sm, m1R (purl), p4, [k1, p6] twice, k1, p16, k2.

Row 17: P2, [k2, C4F, k4, C4B, k2] (row 3 of cable A), p1, [k6, p1] twice, k5, m1R, sm, p1, m1L, k5, [p1, k6] twice, p1, [k2, C4F, k4, C4B, k2] (row 3 of cable A), p1, k12, p1, [k2, C4F, k4, C4B, k2] (row 3 of cable A), p1, [k6, p1] twice, k5, m1R, p1, sm, m1L, k5, [p1, k6] twice, p1, [k2, C4F, k4, C4B, k2] (row 3 of cable A), p2.

Row 18: K2, work row 4 of cable A, k1, [work row 8 of cable C, k1] twice, p6, m1L, sm, k1, m1R, p6, [k1, work row 8 of cable B] twice, k1, work row 4 of cable A, k1, work row 8 of cables B and C, k1, work row 4 of cable A, k1, [work row 8 of cable C, k1] twice, p6, m1L, k1, sm, m1R, p6, [k1, work row 8 of cable B] twice, k1, work row 4 of cable A, k2.

Size 1 only: Shoulder Increases are completed, continue with **Left Front.** *172 sts.*

Size 2 will work all increases as rev St st increases, all cables are now established for the body. Continue increases for Size 2 as follows:

Size 2 – Row 19: P2, work row 5 of cable A, p1, [work row 1 of cable B, p1] three times, m1R (purl), sm, p1, m1L (purl), [p1, work row 1 of cable C] three times, p1, work row 5 of cable A, p1, work row 1 of cables C and B, p1, work row 5 of cable A, p1, [work row 1 of cable B, p1] three times, m1R (purl), p1, sm, m1L (purl), [p1, work row 1 of cable C] three times, p1, work row 5 of cable A, p2.

Size 2 – Row 20: K2, work the next row of cable A, k1, [work the next row of cable C, k1] three times, k to m, m1L, sm, k1, m1R, knit to cable, [work the next row of cable B, k1] three times, work the next row of cable A, k1, work the next row of cables B and C, k1, work the next row of cable A, [k1, work the next row of cable C] three times, k to 1 st before m, m1L, k1, sm, m1R, knit to 1 st before cable, [k1, work the next row of cable B] three times, k1, work the next row of cable A, k2.

Size 2 – Row 21: P2, work the next row of cable A, [p1, work the next row of cable B] three times, p to m, m1R (purl), sm, p1, m1L (purl), p to cable, [work the next row of cable C, p1] three times, work the next row of cable A, p1, work the next row of cables C and B, p1, work the next row of cable A, p1, [work the next row of cable B, p1] three times, p to 1 st before m, m1R (purl), p1, sm, m1L (purl), p to cable, [work the next row of cable C, p1] three times, work the next row of cable A, p2.

Size 2: Repeat **Rows 20-21** once more and work **Row 20** once after the repeat. Shoulder Increases are then completed, continue with **Left Front**. *196 sts.*

Sizes - (-, 3, 4, 5, 6, 7, 8, 9) continue with increases as follows:

Row 19: P2, work row 5 of cable A, p1, [work row 1 of cable B, p1] three times, m1R, sm, p1, m1L, [p1, work row 1 of cable C] three times, p1, work row 5 of cable A, p1, work row 1 of cables C and B, p1, work row 5 of cable A, p1, [work row 1 of cable B, p1] three times, m1R, p1, sm, m1L, [p1, work row 1 of cable C] three times, p1, work row 5 of cable A, p2.

Row 20: K2, work row 6 of cable A, k1, [work row 2 of cable C, k1] three times, p1, m1L (purl), sm, k1, m1R (purl), p1, [work row 2 of cable B, k1] three times, work row 6 of cable A, k1, work row 2 of cables B and C, k1, work row 6 of cable A, [k1, work row 2 of cable C] three times, k1, p1, m1L (purl), k1, sm, m1R (purl), p1, [k1, work row 2 of cable B] three times, k1, work row 6 of cable A, k2.

Row 21: P2, work the next row of cable A, p1, [work the next row of cable B, p1] three times, k2, m1R, sm, p1, m1L, k2, [p1, work the next row of cable C] three times, p1, work the next row of cable A, p1, work the next row of cables C and B, p1, work the next row of cable A, p1, [work the next row of cable B, p1] three times, k2, m1R, p1, sm, m1L, k2, [p1, work the next row of

cable C] three times, p1, work the next row of cable A, p2.

Row 22: K2, work the next row of cable A, k1, [work the next row of cable C, k1] three times, p3, m1L (purl), sm, k1, m1R (purl), p3, k1, [work the next row of cable B, k1] three times, work the next row of cable A, k1, work the next row of cables B and C, k1, work the next row of cable A, [k1, work the next row of cable C] three times, k1, p3, m1L (purl), k1, sm, m1R (purl), p3, [k1, work the next row of cable B] three times, k1, work the next row of cable A, k2.

Row 23: P2, work the next row of cable A, p1, [work the next row of cable B, p1] three times, k4, m1R, sm, p1, m1L, k4, [p1, work the next row of cable C] three times, p1, work the next row of cable A, p1, work the next row of cables C and B, p1, work the next row of cable A, p1, [work the next row of cable B, p1] three times, k4, m1R, p1, sm, m1L, k4, [p1, work the next row of cable C] three times, p1, work the next row of cable A, p2.

Row 24: K2, work the next row of cable A, k1, [work the next row of cable C, k1] three times, p5, m1L (purl), sm, k1, m1R (purl), p5, k1, [work the next row of cable B, k1] three times, work the next row of cable A, k1, work the next row of cables B and C, k1, work the next row of cable A, [k1, work the next row of cable C] three times, k1, p5, m1L (purl), k1, sm, m1R (purl), p5, [k1, work the next row of cable B] three times, k1, work the next row of cable A, k2.

Row 25: P2, work the next row of cable A, [p1, work the next row of cable B] four times, m1R (purl), sm, p1, m1L (purl), [work the next row of cable C, p1] four times, work the next row of cable A, p1, work the next row of cables C and B, p1, work the next row of cable A, [p1, work the next row of cable B] four times, m1R (purl), p1, sm, m1L (purl), [work the next row of cable C, p1] four times, work the next row of cable A, p2.

Row 26: K2, work the next row of cable

A, k1, [work the next row of cable C, k1] four times, m1L (purl) / **sizes 3 and 4:** m1L, sm, k1, m1R (purl) / **sizes 3 and 4:** m1R, k1, [work the next row of cable B, k1] four times, work the next row of cable A, k1, work the next row of cables B and C, k1, work the next row of cable A, [k1, work the next row of cable C] four times, k1, m1L (purl) / **sizes 3 and 4:** m1L, k1, sm, m1R (purl) / **sizes 3 and 4:** m1R, [k1, work the next row of cable B] four times, k1, work the next row of cable A, k2.

Sizes 3 and 4 will work all remaining increases as rev St st increases, all cables are now established for the body. Continue increases as follows:

Sizes 3 and 4 – Row 27: P2, work the next row of cable A, [p1, work the next row of cable B] four times, p to m, m1R (purl), sm, p1, m1L (purl), p to cable, [work the next row of cable C, p1] four times, work the next row of cable A, p1, work the next row of cables C and B, p1, work the next row of cable A, [p1, work the next row of cable B] four times, p to 1 st before m, m1R (purl), p1, sm, m1L (purl), p to cable, [work the next row of cable C, p1] four times, work the next row of cable A, p2.

Sizes 3 and 4 - Row 28: K2, work the next row of cable A, [k1, work the next row of cable C] four times, knit to m, m1L, sm, k1, m1R, k to cable, [work the next row of cable B, k1] four times, work the next row of cable A, k1, work the next row of cables B and C, k1, work the next row of cable A, [k1, work the next row of cable C] four times, k to 1 st before m, m1L, k1, sm, m1R, k to cable, [work the next row of cable B, k1] four times, work the next row of cable A, k2.

Size 3: Shoulder Increases are completed, continue with **Left Front**. *212 sts.*

Size 4: Repeat **Rows 27-28** 2 more times. Then work **Row 27** once more and work **Row 28** once without increases. Shoulder Increases are completed, continue with **Left Front**. *232 sts.*

Sizes - (-, -, -, 5, 6, 7, 8, 9) continue with increases as follows:

Row 27: P2, work the next row of cable A, p1, [work the next row of cable B, p1] four times, k to m, m1R, sm, p1, m1L, k to 1 st before cable, p1, [work the next row of cable C, p1] four times, work the next row of cable A, p1, work the next row of cables C and B, p1, work the next row of cable A, [p1, work the next row of cable B] four times, p1, k to 1 st before m, m1R, p1, sm, m1L, k to 1 st before cable, p1, [work the next row of cable C, p1] four times, work the next row of cable A, p2.

Row 28: K2, work the next row of cable A, [k1, work the next row of cable C] four times, k1, p to m, m1L (purl), sm, k1, m1R (purl), p to 1 st before cable, k1, [work the next row of cable B, k1] four times, work the next row of cable A, k1, work the next row of cables B and C, k1, work the next row of cable A, [k1, work the next row of cable C] four times, k1, p to 1 st before m, m1L (purl), k1, sm, m1R (purl), p to 1 st before cable, k1, [work the next row of cable B, k1] four times, work the next row of cable A, k2.

Row 29: As Row 27.

Row 30: As Row 28.

Row 31: As Row 27.

Row 32: K2, work the next row of cable A, [k1, work the next row of cable C] five times, m1L, sm, k1, m1R, [work the next row of cable B, k1] five times, work the next row of cable A, k1, work the next row of cables B and C, k1, work the next row of cable A, [k1, work the next row of cable C] five times, m1L, k1, sm, m1R, [work the next row of cable B, k1] five times, work the next row of cable A, k2.

Sizes 5 and 6 will work all remaining increases as rev St st increases, all cables are now established for the body. Continue increases as follows:

Sizes 5 and 6 – Row 33: P2, work the next row of cable A, [p1, work the next row of cable B] five times, p to m, m1R (purl), sm, p1, m1L (purl), p to cable, [work the next row of cable C, p1] five times, work the next row of cable A, p1, work the next row of cables C and B, p1, work the next row of cable A, [p1, work the next row of cable B] five times, p to 1 st before m, m1R (purl), p1, sm, m1L (purl), p to cable, [work the next row of cable C, p1] five times, work the next row of cable A, p2.

Sizes 5 and 6 - Row 34: K2, work the next row of cable A, [k1, work the next row of cable C] five times, knit to m, m1L, sm, k1, m1R, k to cable, [work the next row of cable B, k1] five times, work the next row of cable A, k1, work the next row of cables B and C, k1, work the next row of cable A, [k1, work the next row of cable C] five times, k to 1 st before m, m1L, k1, sm, m1R, k to cable, [work the next row of cable B, k1] five times, work the next row of cable A, k2.

Size 5: Repeat **Rows 33-34** 2 more times. Shoulder Increases are completed, continue with **Left Front**. *252 sts.*

Size 6: Repeat **Rows 33-34** 4 more times. Then work **Row 33** once more and work **Row 34** once without increases. Shoulder Increases are completed, continue with **Left Front**. *272 sts.*

Sizes - (-, -, -, -, -, 7, 8, 9) continue with increases as follows:

Row 33: P2, work the next row of cable A, p1, [work the next row of cable B, p1] five times, m1R, sm, p1, m1L, p1, [work the next row of cable C, p1] five times, work the next row of cable A, p1, work the next row of cables C and B, p1, work the next row of cable A, [p1, work the next row of cable B] five times, p1, m1R, p1, sm, m1L, p1, [work the next row of cable C, p1] five times, work the next row of cable A, p2.

Row 34: K2, work the next row of cable A, [k1, work the next row of cable C] five times, k1, p1, m1L (purl), sm, k1, m1R (purl), p1, k1, [work the next row of cable B, k1] five times, work the next row of cable A, k1, work the next row of cables B and C, k1, work the next row of cable A, [k1, work the next row of cable C] five times, k1, p1, m1L (purl), k1,

sm, m1R (purl), p1, k1, [work the next row of cable B, k1] five times, work the next row of cable A, k2.

Row 35: P2, work the next row of cable A, p1, [work the next row of cable B, p1] five times, k to m, m1R, sm, p1, m1L, k to 1 st before cable, p1, [work the next row of cable C, p1] five times, work the next row of cable A, p1, work the next row of cables C and B, p1, work the next row of cable A, [p1, work the next row of cable B] five times, p1, k to 1 st before m, m1R, p1, sm, m1L, k to 1 st before cable, p1, [work the next row of cable C, p1] five times, work the next row of cable A, p2.

Row 36: K2, work the next row of cable A, [k1, work the next row of cable C] five times, k1, p to m, m1L (purl), sm, k1, m1R (purl), p to 1 st before cable, k1, [work the next row of cable B, k1] five times, work the next row of cable A, k1, work the next row of cables B and C, k1, work the next row of cable A, [k1, work the next row of cable C] five times, k1, p to 1 st before m, m1L (purl), k1, sm, m1R (purl), p to 1 st before cable, k1, [work the next row of cable B, k1] five times, work the next row of cable A, k2.

Row 37: As Row 35.

Row 38: As Row 36,

Sizes 7 and 8 will work all remaining increases as rev St st increases, all cables are now established for the body. Continue increases as follows:

Sizes 7 and 8 – Row 39: P2, work the next row of cable A, [p1, work the next row of cable B] six times, p to m, m1R (purl), sm, p1, m1L (purl), p to cable, [work the next row of cable C, p1] six times, work the next row of cable A, p1, work the next row of cables C and B, p1, work the next row of cable A, [p1, work the next row of cable B] six times, p to 1 st before m, m1R (purl), p1, sm, m1L (purl), p to cable, [work the next row of cable C, p1] six times, work the next row of cable A, p2.

Sizes 7 and 8 - Row 40: K2, work the next row of cable A, [k1, work the next row of cable C] six times, knit to m, m1L, sm, k1, m1R, k to cable, [work the next row of cable B, k1] six times, work the next row of cable A, k1, work the next row of cables B and C, k1, work the next row of cable A, [k1, work the next row of cable C] six times, k to 1 st before m, m1L, k1, sm, m1R, k to cable, [work the next row of cable B, k1] six times, work the next row of cable A, k2.

Size 7: Repeat **Rows 39 and 40** 4 more times. Shoulder Increases are completed, continue with **Left Front**. *292 sts.*

Size 8: Repeat **Rows 39-40** 6 more times. Then work **Row 39** once more and work **Row 40** once without increases. Shoulder Increases are completed, continue with **Left Front**. *312 sts.*

Size 9 continue with increases as follows:

Row 39: P2, work the next row of cable A, [p1, work the next row of cable B] six times, m1R (purl), sm, p1, m1L (purl), [work the next row of cable C, p1] six times, work the next row of cable A, p1, work the next row of cables C and B, p1, work the next row of cable A, [p1, work the next row of cable B] six times, m1R (purl), p1, sm, m1L (purl), [work the next row of cable C, p1] six times, work the next row of cable A, p2.

Row 40: K2, work the next row of cable A, [k1, work the next row of cable C] six times, k1, m1L (purl), sm, k1, m1R (purl), k1, [work the next row of cable B, k1] six times, work the next row of cable A, k1, work the next row of cables B and C, k1, work the next row of cable A, [k1, work the next row of cable C] six times, k1, m1L (purl), k1, sm, m1R (purl), k1, [work the next row of cable B, k1] six times, work the next row of cable A, k2.

Row 41: P2, work the next row of cable A, [p1, work the next row of cable B] six times, p1, k to m, m1R, sm, p1, m1L, k to 1 st before cable, p1, [work the next row of cable C, p1] six times, work the next row of cable A, p1, work the next row of cables

C and B, p1, work the next row of cable A, [p1, work the next row of cable B] six times, p1, k to 1 st before m, m1R, p1, sm, m1L, k to 1 st before cable, p1, [work the next row of cable C, p1] six times, work the next row of cable A, p2.

Row 42: K2, work the next row of cable A, [k1, work the next row of cable C] six times, k1, p to cable, m1L (purl), sm, k1, m1R (purl), p to 1 st before cable, k1, [work the next row of cable B, k1] six times, work the next row of cable A, k1, work the next row of cables B and C, k1, work the next row of cable A, [k1, work the next row of cable C] six times, k1, p to 1 st before m, m1L (purl), k1, sm, m1R (purl), p to 1 st before cable, k1, [work the next row of cable B, k1] six times, work the next row of cable A, k2.

Row 43: As Row 41.

Row 44: As Row 42.

Row 45: As Row 41.

Row 46: K2, work the next row of cable A, [k1, work the next row of cable C] seven times, m1L, sm, k1, m1R, [work the next row of cable B, k1] seven times, work the next row of cable A, k1, work the next row of cables B and C, k1, work the next row of cable A, [k1, work the next row of cable C] seven times, m1L, k1, sm, m1R, [work the next row of cable B, k1] seven times, work the next row of cable A, k2.

Size 9 will work all remaining increases as rev St st increases, all cables are now established for the body. Continue increases as follows:

Row 47: P2, work the next row of cable A, [p1, work the next row of cable B] seven times, p to m, m1R (purl), sm, p1, m1L (purl), p to cable, [work the next row of cable C, p1] seven times, work the next row of cable A, p1, work the next row of cables C and B, p1, work the next row of cable A, [p1, work the next row of cable B] seven times, p to 1 st before m, m1R (purl), p1, sm, m1L (purl), p to cable, [work the next row of cable C, p1] seven times, work the next row of cable A, p2.

Row 48: K2, work the next row of cable A, [k1, work the next row of cable C] seven times, knit to m, m1L, sm, k1, m1R, k to cable, [work the next row of cable B, k1] seven times, work the next row of cable A, k1, work the next row of cables B and C, k1, work the next row of cable A, [k1, work the next row of cable C] seven times, k to 1 st before m, m1L, k1, sm, m1R, k to cable, [work the next row of cable B, k1] seven times, work the next row of cable A, k2.

Size 9: Repeat **Rows 47-48** 5 more times. Shoulder Increases are completed, continue with **Left Front**.

All Sizes: Make a note of the last cable row worked, you will need to remember that when you divide for fronts and back.

After all shoulder increases, you should have 172 (196, 212, 232, 252, 272, 292, 312, 332) sts on needle:

- *40 (45, 50, 55, 60, 65, 70, 75, 80) sts for each Left and Right Front and cables as follows: Once cable A, 3 (3, 4, 4, 5, 5, 6, 6, 7) times side cables C/B (cable C on right front, cable B on left front).*
- *90 (100, 110, 120, 130, 140, 150, 160, 170) sts for Back (center stitches between markers) and cables as follows: 3 (3, 4, 4, 5, 5, 6, 6, 7) times cable C, once cable A, cable C and B together, once cable A and 3 (3, 4, 4, 5, 5, 6, 6, 7) times cable C.*
- *2 sts in rev St st for shoulder seam.*

LEFT FRONT

Continue with stitches before first marker, Left Front stitches, only. *Note: Remove the marker and place the following rev St st stitch on holder for sleeve. You can place the back and right front stitches on holder too if desired.*

Next Row (RS): P2, work the next row of cable A, p1, [work the next row of cable B, p1] 3 (3, 4, 4, 5, 5, 6, 6, 7) times, purl to end of left front stitches.

Next Row (WS): Knit to 1 st before cable, [k1, the next row of cable B] 3 (3, 4, 4, 5, 5, 6, 6, 7) times, k1, work the next row of cable A, k2.

Repeat these two rows until the piece measures 6 (6½, 7¼, 7¾, 8½, 9½, 10, 10½, 11)" [15 (16.5, 18, 19, 21, 23, 25, 26, 27) cm] from the end of shoulder increases , ending with a WS row. Cut yarn and place stitches on holder/ waste yarn.

BACK

Continue with Back stitches only. *Note: Remove the marker after the back sts and place the rev St st stitch between increases on holder for sleeve.*

Next Row (RS): Purl to cable, [work the next row of cable C, p1] 3 (3, 4, 4, 5, 5, 6, 6, 7) times, work the next row of cable A, p1, work the next row of cables C and B, p1, work the next row of cable A, [p1, work the next row of cable B] 3 (3, 4, 4, 5, 5, 6, 6, 7) times, purl to end of back stitches.

Next Row (WS): Knit to cable, [work the next row of cable B, k1] 3 (3, 4, 4, 5, 5, 6, 6, 7) times, work the next row of cable A, k1, work the next row of cables B and C, k1, work the next row of cable A, [k1, work the next row of cable C] 3 (3, 4, 4, 5, 5, 6, 6, 7) times, knit to end of back stitches.

Repeat these two rows until the piece measures 6 (6½, 7¼, 7¾, 8½, 9½, 10, 10½, 11)" [15 (16.5, 18, 19, 21, 23, 25, 26, 27) cm] from the end of shoulder increases , ending with a WS row. Cut yarn and place stitches on holder/ waste yarn.

RIGHT FRONT

Continue with Right Front stitches only. Attach yarn to sts on RS.

Next Row (RS): Purl to first cable, [work the next row of cable C, p1] 3 (3, 4, 4, 5, 5, 6, 6, 7) times, work the next row of cable A, p2.

Next Row (WS): K2, work the next row of cable A, k1, [work the next row of cable B, k1] 3 (3, 4, 4, 5, 5, 6, 6, 7) times, knit to end of front sts.

Repeat these two rows until the piece measures 6 (6½, 7¼, 7¾, 8½, 9½, 10, 10½, 11)" [15 (16.5, 18, 19, 21, 23, 25, 26, 27) cm] from the end of shoulder increases , ending with a WS row. Cut yarn.

LOWER BODY

Re-attach yarn to Left Front stitches. Join all parts as follows:

Joining Row (RS): P2, work the next row of cable A, p1, [work the next row of cable B, p1] 3 (3, 4, 4, 5, 5, 6, 6, 7) times, purl to end of left front stitches, pm, work back sts: purl to cable, [work the next row of cable C, p1] 3 (3, 4, 4, 5, 5, 6, 6, 7) times, work the next row of cable A, p1, work the next row of cables C and B, p1, work the next row of cable A, [p1, work the next row of cable B] 3 (3, 4, 4, 5, 5, 6, 6, 7) times, purl to end of back stitches, pm, work Right Front sts: purl to first cable [work the next row of cable C, p1] 3 (3, 4, 4, 5, 5, 6, 6, 7) times, work the next row of cable A, p2.

Next Row (WS): K2, work the next row of cable A, k1, [work the next row of cable B, k1] 3 (3, 4, 4, 5, 5, 6, 6, 7) times, knit to m, sm, knit to cable, [work the next row of cable B, k1] 3 (3, 4, 4, 5, 5, 6, 6, 7) times, work the next row of cable A, k1, work the next row of cables B and C, k1, work the next row of cable A, [k1, work the next row of cable C] 3 (3, 4, 4, 5, 5, 6, 6, 7) times, knit to m, sm, knit to 1 st before cable, [k1, work the next row of cable B] 3 (3, 4, 4, 5, 5, 6, 6, 7) times, k1, work the next row of cable A, k2.

Next Row (RS): P2, the next row of cable A, p1, [work the next row of cable B, p1] 3 (3, 4, 4, 5, 5, 6, 6, 7) times, purl to m, sm, purl to cable, [work the next row 1 of cable C, p1] 3 (3, 4, 4, 5, 5, 6, 6, 7) times, work the next row of cable A, p1, work the next row of cables C and B, p1, work the next row of cable A, [p1, work the next row of cable B] 3 (3, 4, 4, 5, 5, 6, 6, 7) times, purl to m, sm, purl to first cable, [work the next row of cable C, p1] 3 (3, 4, 4, 5, 5, 6, 6, 7) times, work the next row of cable A, p2.

Repeat the last two rows until the body measures 12" [30 cm] from the underarm. Then change to smaller needles and work 2" [5 cm] in garter st. BO body sts on next RS row.

SLEEVES

Using larger needles pick up and knit 29 (32, 35, 38, 42, 46, 49, 52, 54) sts up from underarm to top of shoulder, knit the shoulder st from holder, pick up and knit 30 (33, 36, 39, 43, 47, 50, 53, 55) sts down from top of shoulder to underarm. *You should have 60 (66, 72, 78, 86, 94, 100, 106, 110) sts on needles.* Pm for BOR and join in round. Begin cable pattern as follows:

Setup Round (RS): Sm, purl 9 (12, 15, 11, 15, 12, 15, 18, 20), [p1, work Row 1 of cable B] 3 (3, 3, 4, 4, 5, 5, 5, 5) times, [work Row 1 of cable C, p1] 3 (3, 3, 4, 4, 5, 5, 5, 5) times, purl to end.

Next Round (RS): Sm, purl to 1 st before cable, [p1, work the next row of cable B] 3 (3, 3, 4, 4, 5, 5, 5, 5) times, [work the next row 1 of cable C, p1] 3 (3, 3, 4, 4, 5, 5, 5, 5) times, purl to end.

Repeat the last Round until sleeve measures 4" [10 cm]. Then begin decreases.

Decrease Round (RS): Sm, p2tog, purl to 1 st before cable, [p1, work the next row of cable B] 3 (3, 3, 4, 4, 5, 5, 5) times, [work the next row 1 of cable C] 3 (3, 3, 4, 4, 5, 5, 5) times, purl to last 2 sts, ssp.

Repeat **Decrease Round** on every 10 (10, 10, 8, 8, 7, 7, 6, 6)th round 5 (5, 6, 7, 7, 8, 8, 9, 9) more times.

Continue as established without any further decreases until the sleeve measures 16½" [42 cm]. Then change to smaller needles and work 2" [5 cm] in garter st. BO sleeve stitches on next knit round.

BUTTON BAND

Right Front: Using smaller needles and starting from bottom corner, pick up and knit

100 (104, 108, 112, 116, 120, 124, 128, 132) sts from the right front edge. *Note: If your row gauge differs, pick up sts in approx. ratio of 3 sts every 4 rows.*

Work ¾" [2 cm] in garter st. Make buttonholes on next RS row: Knit 6 (5, 4, 7, 6, 6, 9, 8, 7), work [yo, k2tog, k16 (17, 18, 18, 19, 20, 20, 21, 22)] 5 times, yo, k2tog, knit to end. Continue 1¼" [3 cm] in garter st. BO button band sts.

Left Front: Using smaller needles and starting from the neck corner, pick up and knit 100 (104, 108, 112, 116, 120, 124, 128, 132) sts from the left front edge, same amount as on Right Front. Work 2" [5 cm] in garter st. BO button band sts.

FINISHING

Weave in all yarn ends. Sew on buttons. Block the cardigan to measurements using your preferred method.

Cable A

16 15 14 13 12 11 10 9 8 7 6 5 4 3 2 1

Rows: 6 5 4 3 2 1

Cable B

6 5 4 3 2 1

Rows: 8 7 6 5 4 3 2 1

Cable C

6 5 4 3 2 1

Rows: 8 7 6 5 4 3 2 1

C6B

C6F

C4B

C4F

ROOT

Where do we go from here? When day after day, week after week, all we see is the same wall, the same doorstep, that same view from the old window. But then I remember: this is my home, this is my shelter. These walls are my roots, my background, and these walls keep me safe.

I'm counting the days until we meet again. Yet I have no number, no certainty. I dream and I dread. What if the day never comes? Where do we go from there? Not knowing is the hardest part. Then I see you on my screen and I'm happy. We talk and laugh and maybe cry a little, but we are together. This is also my shelter. My friends and family are *another set of roots*, keeping me safe and helping me grow.

So I reach out with the means I have and I try to help others find that same hope. I do my best knowing that I'm fortunate to have this home, this shelter. It also gives me strength to grow. I'm not perfect and I never will be. But I will always do my best. So I keep hoping and working on the things I can work on.

Hope is something we hold on to. It's the hope that grows from the roots. I know that I'm safe and I'm loved. No matter how long it takes, I will always have hope. So I imagine seeing you again, feeling all the hugs and the mere thought is making my heart sing. Until that day is here, have faith!

ROOT

CABIN LIFE CARDIGAN

SIENNA BEANIE

CABIN LIFE CARDIGAN

by Joji Locatelli

I am a city girl. Born in the city, grown in the city, stuck in the city... How is it possible, then, that every time I've been up on the mountains, I've felt that's where I really belong? Where my heart pumps faster, where my lungs breathe deeper.

Not every dream is meant to be chased after and I know I wouldn't change my life in the city with my little family for anything. But when I close my eyes and I dream of the perfect setting, my mind flies to a log cabin, lost at the end of a winding road up on a cliff.

It is no surprise then, that when I dream of the perfect knit, I always think of garments that I would wear in that imaginary life. Warm, cozy, natural knits. Rustic, full of cables, timeless heirlooms.

This cardigan is knit from the top down. The construction starts at the shoulders, first the back and then the fronts. All the pieces are joined at underarm and then continued in one piece. The sleeves are picked up and knit in the round. It features a shawl collar and I included instructions for optional patch pockets (not photographed) that can be sewn to the garment once blocked... because cabin life requires them!

CABIN LIFE CARDIGAN

SIZES

1 (2, 3, 4, 5, 6, 7, 8, 9). Shown in size 3 on a 36" bust.

Finished bust circumference: 34½ (38½, 42½, 47¼, 50, 55½, 58¾, 62½, 66¾)" [86 (96, 106, 118, 125, 139, 147, 156, 167) cm]. Recommended ease: 4-8" [10-20 cm] of positive ease. See schematics below or more finished measurements at the end of the pattern.

MATERIALS

Yarn: 7 (8, 9, 9, 10, 10, 11, 11, 12) skeins of Nest Worsted by Magpie Fibers (100% Corriedale Wool; 210 yds [192 m] / 100 g) or approx. 1575 (1680, 1785, 1890, 1995, 2100, 2205, 2310, 2415) yds [1440 (1536, 1632, 1728, 1824, 1920, 2016, 2112, 2208) m] of worsted weight yarn. Sample shown in colorway Twilight Honey.

Needles: US 7 [4.5 mm] circular needles, at least 32" [80 cm] long, and US 6 [4 mm] dpns or circular needles.

Other: 1 button, approx 5/8" [2 cm], stitch markers, stitch holders or waste yarn, tapestry needle.

GAUGE

23 sts and 24 rows = 4" [10 cm] in Cabled pattern on US 7 [4.5 mm] needles.

17.5 sts and 24 rows = 4" [10 cm] in Stockinette st on US 7 [4.5 mm] needles. *Before you measure, please take the time to wash and block your swatch in the same manner that you will wash and block your sweater.*

FINISHED MEASUREMENTS

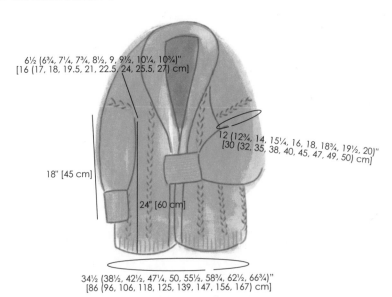

6½ (6¾, 7¼, 7¾, 8½, 9, 9½, 10¼, 10¾)"
[16 (17, 18, 19.5, 21, 22.5, 24, 25.5, 27) cm]

12 (12¾, 14, 15¼, 16, 18, 18¾, 19½, 20)"
[30 (32, 35, 38, 40, 45, 47, 49, 50) cm]

18" [45 cm]

24" [60 cm]

34½ (38½, 42½, 47¼, 50, 55½, 58¾, 62½, 66¾)"
[86 (96, 106, 118, 125, 139, 147, 156, 167) cm]

CABIN LIFE CARDIGAN

STITCHES USED

CABLE LEFT

Row 1: K6

Rows 2 and 4: P6

Row 3: C6F (slip 3 onto CN and hold in front, k3, k3 from CN)

Repeat **Rows 1-4** for pattern.

CABLE RIGHT

Row 1: K6

Rows 2 and 4: P6

Row 3: C6B (slip 3 onto CN and hold in back, k3, k3 from CN)

Repeat **Rows 1-4** for pattern.

INSTRUCTIONS

RIGHT BACK SHOULDER

With US 7 [4.5mm] needles, CO 36 (44, 47, 55, 58, 66, 71, 75, 80) sts.

Set-up row:

Size 1: K5, pm, p6, pm, k10, pm, p6, pm, k9.

Size 2 (3, 4, 5): K4 (5, 6, 6), pm, p6, pm, k8 (9, 11, 12), pm, p6, pm, k8 (9, 11, 12), pm, p6, pm, k6 (6, 9, 10).

Size 6 (7): K5 (6), pm, p6, pm, k10 (11), pm, p6, pm, k10 (11), pm, p6, pm, k10 (11), pm, p6, pm, k7 (8).

Size 8 (9): K5 (5), pm, p6, pm, k9 (10), pm, p6, pm, k9 (10), pm, p6, pm, k9 (10), pm, p6, k9 (10), pm, p6, pm, k4 (5).

Row 1: P3, wrap next st and turn (W&T, see Glossary).

Row 2: K to end.

Break yarn and put all sts on hold (make sure you transfer all the markers).

LEFT BACK SHOULDER

With US 7 [4.5mm] needles, CO 36 (44, 47, 55, 58, 66, 71, 75, 80) sts.

Size 1: K9, pm, p6, pm, k10, pm, p6, pm, k5.

Size 2 (3, 4, 5): K6 (6, 9, 10), pm, p6, pm, k8 (9, 11, 12), pm, p6, pm, k8 (9, 11, 12), pm, p6, pm, k4 (5, 6, 6).

Size 6 (7): K7 (8), pm, p6, pm, k10 (11), pm, p6, pm, k10 (11), pm, p6, pm, k10 (11), pm, p6, k5 (6).

Size 8 (9): K4 (5), pm, p6, pm, k9 (10), pm, p6, pm, k9 (10), pm, p6, pm, k9 (10), pm, p6, k9 (10), pm, p6, k5 (5).

Row 1: Work in patt to end (knit the knit sts and purl the purl sts, slipping markers).

Row 2: K3, W&T.

SHOULDER SHAPING

For the shoulder shaping (both back and front), you don't need to pick up the wraps because they are done over a purl stitch (when seen from the RS).

Row 1: Work in patt to end, CO 24 (24, 27, 27, 28, 28, 29, 31, 32) sts. Place the sts you had on hold for the right shoulder on the left needle. P to first marker, sm, k6, sm, W&T.

You should have 96 (112, 121, 137, 144, 160, 171, 181, 192) sts on the needle.

Row 2: Sm, p6, sm, k10 (8, 9, 11, 12, 10, 11, 9, 10), pm, p6, sm, k10 (8, 9, 11, 12, 10, 11, 9, 10), pm, p6, sm, k10 (8, 9, 11, 12, 10, 11, 9, 10), sm, p6, sm, W&T.

Row 3: Sm, (k6, sm, p to m, sm) 3 times, k6, sm, p to 1 st from m, W&T.

Row 4: K to m, sm, (p6, sm, k to m, sm) 3 times, p6, sm, k to 1 st from m, W&T.

Row 5: P to m, sm, (C6F, sm, p to m, sm) twice, (C6B, sm, p to m, sm) twice, k6, sm, W&T.

Row 6: Sm, p6, sm, (k to m, sm, p6, sm) 5 times, sm, W&T.

Size 1 only:

Row 7: Sm, (k6, sm, p to m, sm) 5 times, k6, sm, p to end.

Row 8: K to m, sm, (p6, sm, k to m, sm) 5 times, p6, sm, k to end.

Row 9: P to m, sm, (C6F, sm, p to m, sm) 3 times, (C6B, sm, p to m, sm) twice, C6B, sm, p to end.

Row 10: K to m, sm, (p6, sm, k to m, sm) 5 times, p6, sm, k to end.

Move to BACK section.

Sizes 2, 3, 4, 5, 6, 7, 8 and 9 only:

Row 7: Sm, (k6, sm, p to m, sm) 5 times, k6, sm, p to 1 st from m, W&T.

Row 8: K to m, sm, (p6, sm, k to m, sm) 5 times, p6, sm, k to 1 st from m, W&T.

Sizes 2, 3, 4 and 5 only:

Row 9: P to m, sm, (C6F, sm, p to m, sm) 3 times, (C6B, sm, p to m, sm) 3 times, sm, k6, sm, p to end.

Row 10: K to m, sm, (p6, sm, k to m, sm) 7 times, p6, sm, k to end.

Move to BACK section.

Sizes 6, 7, 8 and 9 only:

Row 9: P to m, sm, (C6F, sm, p to m, sm) 3 times, (C6B, sm, p to m, sm) 3 times, sm, k6, sm, W&T.

Row 10: Sm, (p6, sm, k to m, sm) 7 times, p6, sm, W&T.

Row 11: Sm, (k6, sm, p to m, sm) 7 times, k6, sm, p to 1 st from m, W&T.

Row 12: K to m, sm, (p6, sm, k to m, sm) 7 times, p6, sm, k to 1 st from m, W&T.

Sizes 6 and 7 only:

Row 13: P to m, sm, (C6F, sm, p to m, sm) 5 times, (C6B, sm, p to m, sm) 4 times, sm, k6, sm, p to end.

Row 14: K to m, sm, (p6, sm, k to m, sm) 9 times, p6, sm, k to end.

Move to BACK section.

Sizes 8 and 9 only:

Row 13: P to m, sm, (C6F, sm, p to m, sm) 4 times, (C6B, sm, p to m, sm) 3 times, sm, k6, sm, W&T.

Row 14: Sm, (p6, sm, k to m, sm) 9 times, p6, sm, W&T.

Row 15: Sm, (k6, sm, p to m, sm) 9 times, k6, sm, p to 1 st from m, W&T.

Row 16: K to m, sm, (p6, sm, k to m, sm) 9 times, p6, sm, k to 1 st from m, W&T.

Row 17: P to m, sm, (C6F, sm, p to m, sm) 5 times, (C6B, sm, p to m, sm) 4 times, sm, k6, sm, p to end.

Row 18: K to m, sm, (p6, sm, k to m, sm) 11 times, p6, sm, k to end.

Move to BACK section.

BACK

Rows 1 and 3: P to m, sm, (Cable Left, sm, p to m, sm) 3 (4, 4, 4, 4, 5, 5, 6, 6) times, (Cable Right, sm, p to m, sm) 2 (3, 3, 3, 3, 4, 4, 5, 5) times, Cable Right, sm, p to end.

Rows 2 and 4: K to m, sm, (Cable Right, sm, k to m, sm) 3 (4, 4, 4, 4, 5, 5, 6, 6) times, (Cable Left, sm, k to m, sm) 2 (3, 3, 3, 3, 4, 4, 5, 5) times, Cable Left, sm, k to end.

Repeat **Rows 1-4** until work measures 6½ (6¾, 7¼, 7¾, 8½, 9, 9½, 10¼, 10¾)" [16 (17, 18, 19.5, 21, 22.5, 24, 25.5, 27) cm] from the shoulder CO, measured along the sleeve edge, ending with a WS row. Take note of what row of the pattern repeat you ended on so you can knit the fronts to match.

Break yarn and put all sts on hold. Make sure you transfer all the markers as well.

RIGHT FRONT SHOULDER

With RS facing you and US 7 [4.5 mm] needles, pick up and knit 36 (44, 47, 55, 58, 66, 71, 75, 80) sts from the right shoulder cast on.

Set-up row (WS): K9 (6, 6, 9, 10, 7, 8, 4, 5), pm, (p6, pm, k10 (8, 9, 11, 12, 10, 11, 9, 10), pm) 1 (2, 2, 2, 3, 3, 4, 4) times, p6, pm, k to end.

Row 1 (RS): Work in patt to end of row (knit the knit stitches and purl the purl stitches, slipping markers).

Row 2 (WS): K3, W&T.

Row 3: P to end.

Row 4: K to m, sm, p6, sm, W&T.

Row 5 - Neck increase row: Sm, k6, sm, p to 1 st from end, m1L (purl), p1.

Row 6: K to m, sm, p6, sm, k to 1 st from m, W&T.

Row 7: P to m, sm, C6B, sm, p to end.

Row 8: K to m, sm, p6, sm, k to m, sm, p6, sm, W&T.

Size 1 only:

Row 9: Sm, k6, sm, p to m, sm, k6, sm, p to end.

Row 10: (K to m, sm, p6, sm) twice, k to end.

Row 11 - Neck increase row: (P to m, sm, C6B, sm) twice, p to 1 st from end, m1L (purl), p1.

Row 12: (K to m, sm, p6, sm) twice, k to end.

Move to RIGHT FRONT section.

Sizes 2, 3, 4, 5, 6, 7, 8 and 9 only:

Row 9: Sm, k6, sm, p to m, sm, k6, sm, p to end.

Row 10: (K to m, sm, p6, sm) twice, k to 1 st from m, W&T.

Sizes 2, 3, 4 and 5 only:

Row 11 - Neck increase row: (P to m, sm, C6B, sm) twice, p to 1 st from end, m1L (purl), p1.

Row 12: K to m, (sm, p6, sm, k to m) twice, sm, p6, sm, k to end.

Move to RIGHT FRONT section.

Sizes 6, 7, 8 and 9 only:

Row 11 - Neck increase row: (P to m, sm, C6B, sm) twice, p to 1 st from end, m1L (purl), p1.

Row 12: K to m, (sm, p6, sm, k to m) twice, sm, p6, sm, W&T.

Row 13: Sm, k6, (sm, p to m, sm, k6) twice, sm, p to end.

Row 14: (K to m, sm, p6, sm) 3 times, k to 1 st from m, W&T.

Sizes 6 and 7 only:

Row 15: (P to m, sm, C6B, sm) 3 times, p to end.

Row 16: K to m, (sm, p6, sm, k to m) 3 times, sm, p6, sm, k to end.

Move to RIGHT FRONT section

Sizes 8 and 9 only:

Row 15: (P to m, sm, C6B, sm) 3 times, p to end.

Row 16: K to m, (sm, p6, sm, k to m) 3 times, sm, p6, sm, W&T.

Row 17 - Neck increase row: Sm, k6, (sm, p to m, sm, k6) 3 times, sm, p to 1 st from end, m1L (purl), p1.

Row 18: (K to m, sm, p6, sm) 4 times, k to 1 st from m, W&T.

Row 19: (P to m, sm, C6B, sm) 4 times, p to end.

Row 20: K to m, (sm, p6, sm, k to m) 4 times, sm, p6, sm, k to end.

You should have made a total of 2 (2, 2, 2, 2, 2, 2, 3, 3) neck increases. Continue to work a neck increase every 6th following row.

RIGHT FRONT

Row 1: P to m, (sm, Cable Right, sm, p to m) 1 (2, 2, 2, 2, 3, 3, 4, 4) times, sm, Cable right, sm, work in patt to end.

Row 2: K to m, (sm, Cable Right, sm, k to m) 1 (2, 2, 2, 2, 3, 3, 4, 4), sm, Cable Right, sm, k to end.

Continue working in pattern, always working the following row of the Cables and increasing a 'purl' stitch at neck edge every 6th row until you have 11 (9, 10, 12, 13, 11, 12, 10, 11) sts between your last marker and your neck edge.

When it's time to work another neck increase row, work this row instead:

Row 1 (RS) - Neck increase row: Work in patt to 1 st from end, m1L, p1.

Row 2 (WS): K1, p1, pm, k to m, work in patt to end.

Rows 3 and 5: Work in patt to last marker, sm, k1, p1.

Rows 4 and 6: K1, p1, sm, work in patt to end.

Row 7: Work in patt to last marker, sm, k1,

m1L, p1.

Rows 8, 10, 12: K1, p to m, sm, work in patt to end.

Rows 9, 11: Work in patt to last marker, sm, k to 1 st from end, p1.

Row 13: Work in patt to last marker, sm, k to 1 st from end m1L, p1.

Row 14: K1, p to m, sm, work in patt to end.

Read the entire next section before proceeding, it describes all the necessary neck increases. Some sizes will finish the neck increases before joining the body and some sizes will do so after.

Continue working in this manner, increasing 1 'knit' st at each neck edge, every 6th row until you have increased a total of 6 'knit' stitches. As you can see, we are increasing enough stitches here to create a new Cable Right. Once you have 6 'knit' sts in this new column, place a marker and work them as Cable Right, beginning on the same row repeat as the other cables in the front.

Then increase 'purl' stitches again (every 6th row) until you have 5 'purl' stitches between this new marker and the neck edge.

Continue working in this manner until the front measures 6½ (6¾, 7¼, 7¾, 8½, 9, 9½, 10¼, 10¾)" [16 (17, 18, 19.5, 21, 22.5, 24, 25.5, 27) cm] from the shoulder CO, measured along the sleeve edge, ending with the same WS row as you did for the back.

Break yarn and put all sts on hold.

LEFT FRONT SHOULDER

With RS facing you and US 7 [4.5 mm] needles, pick up and knit 36 (44, 47, 55, 58, 66, 71, 75, 80) sts from the left shoulder cast on.

Set-up row (WS): K5 (4, 5, 6, 6, 5, 6, 5, 5), pm, (p6, pm, k10 (8, 9, 11, 12, 10, 11, 9, 10), pm) 1 (2, 2, 2, 2, 3, 3, 4, 4) times, p6, pm, k to end.

Row 1: P3, W&T.

Row 2: K to end.

Row 3: P to m, sm, k6, sm, W&T.

Row 4: Sm, p6, sm, k to end.

Row 5 - Neck increase row: P1, m1R (purl), p to m, sm, k6, sm, p to 1 st from m, W&T.

Row 6: K to m, sm, p6, sm, k to end.

Row 7: P to m, sm, C6F, sm, p to m, sm, k6, sm, W&T.

Row 8: Sm, p6, sm, k to m, sm, p6, sm, k to end.

Size 1 only:

Row 9: (P to m, sm, k6, sm) twice, p to end.

Row 10: (K to m, sm, p6, sm) twice, k to end.

Row 11 - Neck increase row: P1, m1R (purl), (p to m, sm, C6F, sm) twice, p to end.

Row 12: Work in patt to end.

Move to LEFT FRONT section.

Sizes 2, 3, 4, 5, 6, 7, 8 and 9 only:

Row 9: (P to m, sm, k6, sm) twice, p to 1 st from m, W&T.

Row 10: (K to m, sm, p6, sm) twice, k to end.

Sizes 2, 3, 4 and 5 only:

Row 11 - Neck increase row: P1, m1R (purl), p to m, (sm, C6F, sm, p to m) twice, sm, k6, sm, p to end.

Row 12: (K to m, sm, p6, sm) 3 times, k to end.

Move to LEFT FRONT section

Sizes 6, 7, 8 and 9 only:

Row 11 - Neck increase row: P1, m1R (purl), p to m, (sm, C6F, sm, p to m) twice, sm, k6, W&T.

Row 12: P6, sm, (k to m, sm, p6, sm) twice, k to end.

Row 13: (P to m, sm, k6, sm) 3 times, p to 1 st from m, W&T.

Row 14: (K to m, sm, p6, sm) 3 times, k to end.

Sizes 6 and 7 only:

Row 15: P to m, (sm, C6F, sm, p to m) 3 times, sm, k6, sm, p to end.

Row 16: (K to m, sm, p6, sm) 4 times, k to end.

Move to LEFT FRONT section.

Sizes 8 and 9 only:

Row 15: P to m, (sm, C6F, sm, p to m) 3 times, sm, k6, W&T.

Row 16: P6, sm, (k to m, sm, p6, sm) 3 times, k to end.

Row 17 - Neck increase row: P1, m1R (purl), p to m, sm, k6, sm, (P to m, sm, k6, sm) 3 times, p to 1 st from m, W&T.

Row 18: (K to m, sm, p6, sm) 4 times, k to end.

Row 19: P to m, (sm, C6F, sm, p to m) 4 times, sm, k6, sm, p to end.

Row 20: (K to m, sm, p6, sm) 5 times, k to end.

You should have made a total of 2 (2, 2, 2, 2, 2, 2, 3, 3) neck increases. Continue to work a neck increase every 6th following row.

LEFT FRONT

Row 1: Work in patt to m, (sm, Cable Left, sm, p to m) 1 (2, 2, 2, 2, 3, 3, 4, 4) times, sm, Cable Left, sm, p to end.

Row 2: K to m, (sm, Cable Left, sm, k to m) twice, sm, Cable Left, sm, k to end.

Continue working in pattern, always working the following row of the Cables and increasing a 'purl' stitch at neck edge every 6th row until you have 11 (9, 10, 12, 13, 11, 12, 10, 11) sts between your last marker and your neck edge.

When it's time to work another neck increase row, work this row instead:

Row 1 (RS) - Neck increase row: P1, m1R, p to m, sm, work in patt to end.

Row 2 (WS): Work in patt to 2 sts from end, pm, p1, k1.

Rows 3 and 5: P1, k1, p to m, sm, work in patt to end.

Rows 4 and 6 (WS): Work in patt to 2 sts from end, sm, p1, k1.

Row 7: P1, m1R, k1, sm, work in patt to end.

Row 8: Work in patt to last m, sm, p2, k1.

Rows 9, 11: P1, k to m, sm, work in patt to end.

Rows 10, 12, 14: Work in patt to last m, sm, p to 1 st from end, k1.

Row 13: P1, m1R, k to m, sm, work in patt to end.

Read the entire next section before proceeding, it describes all the necessary neck increases. Some sizes will finish the neck increases before joining the body and some sizes will do so after.

Continue working in this manner, increasing 1 'knit' st at each neck edge, every 6th row until you have increased a total of 6 'knit' stitches. As you can see, we are increasing enough stitches here to create a new Cable Left. Once you have 6 'knit' sts in this new column, place a marker and work them as Cable Left, beginning on the same row repeat as the other cables in the front.

Then increase 'purl' stitches again (every 6th row) until you have 5 'purl' stitches between this new marker and the neck edge.

Continue working in this manner until the front measures 6½ (6¾, 7¼, 7¾, 8½, 9, 9½, 10¼, 10¾)" [16 (17, 18, 19.5, 21, 22.5, 24, 25.5, 27) cm] from the shoulder CO, measured along the sleeve edge, ending with the same WS row as you did for the back.

Don't break yarn.

JOIN BODY

Remember to continue working neck increases as described in the front sections.

Next row (RS):

Sizes 1 (2, 5, 6, 9) only: Work the left front sts in patt to end of row. Place the sts you had on hold for the back on the left needle. Work in patt to end of row. Place the sts you had on hold for the right front on the left needle. Work in patt to end of row.

Sizes 3 (4, 7 and 8) only: Work the left front sts in patt to 2 sts before the end of row, p2tog. Place the sts you had on hold for the back on the left needle. Work in patt to 2 sts from end, p2tog. Place the sts you had on hold for the right front on the left needle. Work in patt to end of row.

Next row (WS): Work all sts in pattern.

Continue working in pattern. *When you finish all your front increases you will have a total of 192 (226, 243, 273, 286, 320, 341, 363, 384) sts on the needles.*

Work in pattern until work measures 3¼" [8 cm] from the underarm, ending with Row 4 of the Cable repeats, removing all markers on the last row.

CABLE TRANSITIONS

Sizes 1 (2, 5, 6, 9) - with an even number of sts in-between cables.

Row 1 (RS): P4, [C3B, C3F, p8 (6, 10, 8, 8)] to 12 sts from end, C3B, C3F, p4.

Sizes 3 (4, 7, 8) - with an odd number of sts in-between cables.

Row 1 (RS): P4, [C3B, m1L (purl), C3F, p3 (4, 4, 3), p2tog, p2 (3, 3, 2)] to 12 sts from end, C3B, m1L (purl), C3F, p4.

All sizes:

Row 2: K4, [p3, k2 (2, 3, 3, 2, 2, 3, 3, 2), p3, k8 (6, 6, 8, 10, 8, 8, 6, 8)] to 12 (12, 13, 13, 12, 12, 13, 13, 12) sts from end, p3, k2 (2, 3, 3, 2, 2, 3, 3, 2), p3, k4.

Row 3: P3, [C3B, p2 (2, 3, 3, 2, 2, 3, 3, 2), C3F, p6 (4, 4, 6, 8, 6, 6, 4, 6)] to 13 (13, 14, 14, 13, 13, 14, 14, 13) sts from end, C3B, p2 (2, 3, 3, 2, 2, 3, 3, 2), C3F, p3.

Row 4: K3, [p3, k4 (4, 5, 5, 4, 4, 5, 5, 4), p3, k6 (4, 4, 6, 8, 6, 6, 4, 6)] to 13 (13, 14, 14, 13, 13, 14, 14, 13) sts from end, p3, k4 (4, 5, 5, 4, 4, 5, 5, 4), p3, k3.

Row 5: P2, [C3B, p4 (4, 5, 5, 4, 4, 5, 5, 4), C3F, p4 (2, 2, 4, 6, 4, 4, 2, 4] to 14 (14, 15, 15, 14, 14, 15, 15, 14) sts from end, C3B, p4 (4, 5, 5, 4, 4, 5, 5, 4), C3F, p2.

Row 6: K2, [p3, k6 (6, 7, 7, 6, 6, 7, 7, 6), p3, k4 (2, 2, 4, 6, 4, 4, 2, 4)] to 14 (14, 15, 15, 14, 14, 15, 15, 14) sts from end, p3, k6 (6, 7, 7, 6, 6, 7, 7, 6), p3, k2.

Row 7: P1, [C3B p6 (6, 7, 7, 6, 6, 7, 7, 6), C3F, p2 (0, 0, 2, 4, 2, 2, 0, 2)] to 15 (15, 16, 16, 15, 15, 16, 16, 15) sts from end, C3B, p6 (6, 7, 7, 6, 6, 7, 7, 6), C3F, p1.

Row 8: K1, [p3, k8 (8, 9, 9, 8, 8, 9, 9, 8), p3, k2 (0, 0, 2, 4, 2, 2, 0, 2)] to 15 (15, 16, 16, 15, 15, 16, 16, 15) sts from end, p3, k8 (8, 9, 9, 8, 8, 9, 9, 8), p3, k1.

Sizes 1 (4, 6, 7, 9):

Row 9: P1, sl1 onto CN and hold in back, k2, p1 from CN, p8 (9, 8, 9, 8), C3F, [C3B, p8 (9, 8, 9, 8), C3F] to 16 (17, 16, 17, 16) sts from end, C3B, p to last 4 sts, sl2 onto CN and hold in front, p1, k2 from CN, p1.

Row 10: K1, p2, 10 (11, 10, 11, 10), pm, [p6, pm, k10 (11, 10, 11, 10), pm] to 20 (21, 20, 21, 20) sts from end, p6, pm, k to 3 sts from end, p2, k1.

Row 11: P1, sl1 onto CN and hold in back, k1, p1 from CN, p to m, (C6F, sm, p to m, sm) 6 (8, 10, 10, 12) times, (C6B, sm, p to m, sm) 4 (6, 8, 8, 10) times, C6B, sm, p to 3 sts from end, sl1 onto CN and hold in front, p1, k1 from CN, p1.

Row 12: K to m, sm, p6, (sm, k to m, sm p6) to last m, sm, k to end.

Sizes 2 (3, 8):

Row 9: P1, sl1 onto CN and hold in back, k2, p1 from CN, p9 (10, 10), [pm, C6F, pm, p8 (9, 9)] 8 (8, 12) times, [pm, C6B, pm, p8 (9, 9)] 6 (6, 10) times, pm, C6B, pm, p to 4 sts from end, sl2 onto CN and hold in front, p1, k2 from CN, p1.

Row 10: K1, p2, (k to m, sm, p to m, sm) to last m, k to 3 sts from end, p2, k1.

Row 11: P1, sl1 onto CN and hold in back, k1, p1 from CN, (p to m, sm, k6, sm), to last m, p to 3 sts from end, sl1 onto CN and hold in front, p1, k1 from CN, p1.

Row 12: K to m, sm, p6, (sm, k to m, sm, p6) to last m, sm, k to end.

Size 5:

Row 9: P1, sl1 onto CN and hold in back, k2, p1 from CN, p8, C3F, p2, [C3B p8, C3F, p2] to 16 sts from end, C3B, p8, sl2 onto CN and hold in front, p1, k2 from CN, p1.

Row 10: K1, p2, k10, p3, k2, [p3, k10, p3, k2] to 16 sts from end, p3, k10, p2, k1.

Row 11: P1, sl1 onto CN and hold in back, k1, p1 from CN, p10, C3F, [C3B, p10, C3F] to 17 sts from end, C3B, p10, sl1 onto CN and hold in front, p1, k1 from CN, p1.

Row 12: K14, (pm, p6, pm, k12) to last 20 sts, pm, p6, pm, k to end.

All sizes: You've established your new cabled pattern for the body.

Row 1: P to m, (sm, Cable Left -starting on row 1 of the repeat-, sm, p to m) 6 (8, 8, 8, 8, 10, 10, 12, 12) times, (sm, Cable Right, sm, p to m) 4 (6, 6, 6, 6, 8, 8, 10) times, sm, Cable Right, sm, p to end.

Row 2: K to m, sm, p6, (sm, k to m, sm, p6) to last m, sm, k to end.

Continue working in this manner, repeating **Rows 1-2** and always working the next row of the Cable repeats until work measures 21½" [54 cm] from the armhole, ending with a WS row. On the last row, adjust the stitch count to work the hem:

Sizes 1 and 9: Decrease 2 sts.

Sizes 2 and 5: No changes.

Sizes 3 and 8: Decrease 1 st.

Sizes 4 and 7: Increase 1 st.

Size 6: Increase 2 sts.

You should now have 190 (226, 242, 274, 286, 322, 342, 362, 382) sts.

Switch to US 6 [4 mm] needles.

Next row (RS): K2 (p2, k2) to end of row.

Next row (WS): P2, (k2, p2) to end of row.

Repeat these 2 rows 6 more times. Bind off all sts in pattern.

SLEEVES

With RS facing you, US 7 [4.5 mm] needles and starting at the bottom of the armhole, pick up and knit 52 (56, 62, 66, 70, 78, 82, 86, 92) sts around the armhole. The sleeve is knitted inside out so that the reverse of the Stockinette st is facing the RS of the garment.

Turn work, knit to the end of round. Place marker and join for working in the round (inside out).

Work 10 rounds in stockinette stitch.

Next round - decrease round: K1, ssk, k to 3 sts before the end of round, k2tog, k1.

Continue working in stockinette stitch, repeating a decrease round every 11th

(11th, 10th, 7th, 6th, 5th, 4th, 4th, 4th) following row 5 (5, 6, 8, 10, 12, 14, 14, 15) more times.

You should have 40 (44, 48, 48, 48, 52, 52, 56, 56) sts.

When sleeve measures 13½" [33.5 cm] from the armhole, switch to US 6 [4 mm] needles and start cuff.

Next round: (K2, p2) to end.

Repeat the last round until the cuff measures 4½" [11.5 cm]

Bind off all sts in pattern.

FRONT BANDS AND COLLAR

Before starting the front bands and collar, place 1 safety pin at each front, marking the placement of your last neck increase.

With US 6 [4 mm] needles and starting at the bottom corner of the right front, pick up and knit 92 (93, 92, 95, 95, 98, 99, 99, 100) sts between the bottom edge and the neck increase marker and 52 (52, 56, 56, 58, 58, 60, 64, 66) sts between this point and the shoulder seam. Pm, pickup and knit 26 (26, 29, 29, 30, 30, 31, 33, 34) sts along the back neck, pm. Pick up and knit 52 (52, 56, 56, 58, 58, 60, 64, 66) sts between the shoulder and the other neck increase marker, pick up 92 (93, 92, 95, 95, 98, 99, 99, 100) sts between this point and the end.

These numbers are approximate and you can pick up more or less stitches according to the total length you gave your cardigan. When working a garter stitch band, I usually pick up 5 sts out of every 7 rows.

Row 1 (WS): K to 5 sts before the second marker (don't count the safety pin), W&T.

Row 2 (RS): K to 5 sts before next marker, W&T.

Row 3: K to last wrapped st, knit it (no need to pick up the wrap), k1, W&T.

Repeat **Row 3** 53 (53, 57, 57, 59, 59, 61, 65, 67) more times.

Next 2 rows: K to last wrapped st, knit it, k to end of row (removing markers).

Knit 4 more rows.

Next row - Buttonhole: Knit until 6 sts

before the right neck increase marker, work a 4-st buttonhole as follows:

Bring the yarn forward, slip 1 purlwise, move the yarn back. (Slip another stitch, pass the first slipped st over the second one) 3 times. Slip the stitch left on the right needle and turn work. Now with WS facing you, cable cast on 4 sts (bring the yarn to front in-between stitches before putting the 4th st on the left needle). Turn work. Slip the next stitch pwise, pass the last CO stitch over it. (See Glossary for a link to a tutorial).

Knit to the end of row.

Knit 8 more rows.

Next row (WS): Bind off all sts using a 3 sts i-cord bind off (see Glossary).

PATCH POCKETS

(Optional, not photographed)

Left Pocket

With US 7 [4.5 mm] needles, CO 31 (29, 30, 33, 34, 32, 34, 32, 33) sts.

Setup row (WS): K3 (3, 3, 4, 4, 4, 5, 5, 5), pm, p6, pm, k10 (8, 9, 11, 12, 10, 11, 9, 10), pm, p6, pm, k to end.

Row 1 (RS): P to m, sm, Cable Left, sm, p to m, sm, Cable Left, sm, p to end.

Row 2 (WS): K to m, sm, work next row of Cable Left, sm, k to m, sm, work next row of Cable Left, sm, k to end.

Continue working in the established pattern until the pocket measures 5" [13 cm].

Switch to US 6 [4 mm] needles.

Next row: K4, (k2tog, k4) 4 times, k2tog, k to end.

Knit 10 rows in garter stitch. Bind off all sts using a 3 sts i-cod bind off.

Right Pocket

With US 7 [4.5 mm] needles, CO 31 (29, 30, 33, 34, 32, 34, 32, 33) sts.

Setup row (WS): K6, pm, p6, pm, k10 (8, 9, 11, 12, 10, 11, 9, 10), pm, p6, pm, k to end.

Row 1 (RS): P to m, sm, Cable Right, sm, p to m, sm, Cable Right, sm, p to end.

Row 2 (WS): K to m, sm, work next row of Cable Right, sm, k to m, sm, work next row of Cable Right, sm, k to end.

Continue working in the established pattern until the pocket measures 5" [13 cm].

Switch to US 6 [4 mm] needles.

Next row: K4, (k2tog, k4) 4 times, k2tog, k to end.

Knit 10 rows in garter stitch. Bind off all sts using a 3 sts i-cord bind off.

Position the pockets onto your coat fronts so that the cables on the pockets match the columns of cables on the coat and pin them into place. Sew them carefully using mattress stitch.

FINISHING

Weave in all yarn ends and block the cardigan to measurments using your preferred method. Sew on the patch pockets and the button.

FINISHED MEASUREMENTS

Bust circumference: 34½ (38½, 42½, 47¼, 50, 55½, 58¾, 62½, 66¾)" [86 (96, 106, 118, 125, 139, 147, 156, 167) cm].

Armhole depth: 6½ (6¾, 7¼, 7¾, 8½, 9, 9½, 10¼, 10¾)" [16 (17, 18, 19.5, 21, 22.5, 24, 25.5, 27) cm].

Upper sleeve circumference: 12 (12¾, 14, 15¼, 16, 18, 18¾, 19½, 20)" [30 (32, 35, 38, 40, 45, 47, 49, 50) cm].

Sleeve length from underarm to cuff: 18" [45 cm].

Length from underarm to hem: 24" [60 cm].

SIENNA BEANIE

by Veera Välimäki

An earthy and sweet song of deep ribbing and some bobbles with cables is like a comforting whisper in my ears. With every stitch, I feel the deep connection to Mother Earth and to my own roots. These twists will hopefully make you feel full of happiness and feel more grounded.

Sienna is all about the wonderfully soft and smooth yarn that simply begs to be knitted into cables and bobbles. The beanie is worked from brim up.

SIENNA BEANIE

SIZES

SMALL (MEDIUM, LARGE)

Finished measurements: 18 (20, 22)" [45 (50, 55) cm] in circumference at brim and 13¾" [35 cm] long. Choose a size with approx. 3-4" [8-10 cm] of negative ease.

MATERIALS

Yarn: 1 (2, 2) skein(s) of Aubrey Sport by Martin's Lab (55% SW BFL, 45% Silk; 328 yds [300 m] / 100 g). Approx. 300 (350, 390) yds [280 (320, 360) m] of sport weight yarn. Sample knit in color Fox Tail.

Needles: US 2½ [3 mm] and US 1½ [2.5 mm] circular needles,16" [40 cm] long, and dpns in larger size.

Other: Stitch marker, cable needle and tapestry needle.

GAUGE

30 sts and 38 rows = 4" [10 cm] in cable pattern on US 2½ [3 mm] needles.

32 sts and 38 rows = 4" [10 cm] in 1X1 ribbing, unstretched, on US 1½ [2.5 mm] needles.

Before you measure, please take the time to wash and block your swatch in the same manner that you will wash and block your beanie.

FINISHED MEASUREMENTS

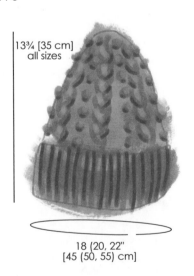

13¾ [35 cm]
all sizes

18 (20, 22"
[45 (50, 55) cm]

SIENNA BEANIE

INSTRUCTIONS

BRIM

Using smaller needles and a tubular CO, CO 144 (160, 176) sts. Carefully join in round without twisting your stitches and place a marker for BOR. Work 5½" [13 cm] in 1X1 ribbing (*k1, p1; repeat from * to end of round).

Increase on following round: Sm, *k9, p1, knit 6, m1L (purl); repeat from * to end. 9 (10, 11) sts increased; you should have 153 (170, 187) sts on the needles.

CABLE PATTERN

Change to larger needles. Begin cable pattern. *Note: See page 54 for chart. Chart row worked 9 (10, 11) times on each round.*

   Round 1 (RS): Sm, *k9, p1, k6, p1; repeat from * to end.

   Round 2: Sm, *C6B, k3, p1, C6F, p1; repeat from * to end.

   Rounds 3, 4 and 5: Sm, *k9, p1, k6, p1; repeat from * to end.

   Round 6: Sm, *k3, C6F, p1, k6, p1; repeat from * to end.

   Round 7: Sm, *k9, p1, k6, p1; repeat from * to end.

   Round 8: Sm, *k9, p1, C6F, p1; repeat from * to end.

   Round 9: Sm, *k9, p1, k6, p1; repeat from * to end.

   Round 10: Sm, *C6B, k3, p1, k6, p1; repeat from * to end.

   Round 11: Sm, *k9, p1, k6, p1; repeat from * to end.

   Round 12: Sm, *k9, p1, k2, MB, k3, p1; repeat from * to end.

   Round 13: Sm, *k9, p1, k6, p1; repeat from * to end.

   Round 14: Sm, *k3, C6F, p1, C6F, p1; repeat from * to end.

   Rounds 15, 16 and 17: Sm, *k9, p1, k6, p1; repeat from * to end.

   Round 18: Sm, *C6B, k3, p1, k6, p1; repeat from * to end.

   Round 19: Sm, *k9, p1, k6, p1; repeat from * to end.

   Round 20: Sm, *k9, p1, C6F, p1; repeat from * to end.

   Round 21: Sm, *k9, p1, k6, p1; repeat from * to end.

   Round 22: Sm, *k3, C6F, p1, k6, p1; repeat from * to end.

   Round 23: Sm, *k9, p1, k6, p1; repeat from * to end.

   Round 24: Sm, *k9, p1, k2, MB, k3, p1; repeat from * to end.

Repeat **Rounds 1-24** one more time. Then work **Rounds 1-5** once.

CROWN DECREASES

Note: See page 54 for chart.

   Round 1: Sm, *k2tog, k1, C6F, p1, k6, p1; repeat from * to end.

   Round 2: Sm, *k8, p1, k6, p1; repeat from * to end.

   Round 3: Sm, *k8, p1, C6F, p1; repeat from * to end.

   Round 4: Sm, *k8, p1, k6, p1; repeat from * to end.

   Round 5: Sm, *C6B, ssk, p1, k6, p1; repeat from * to end.

   Round 6-7: Sm, *k7, p1, k6, p1; repeat from * to end.

   Round 8: Sm, *k2tog, k5, p1, k6, p1; repeat from * to end.

   Round 9: Sm, *C6F, p1, C6F, p1; repeat from * to end.

   Rounds 10: Sm, *k6, p1, k4, p1; repeat from * to end.

Rounds 11-12: Sm, *k6, p1, k5, p1; repeat from * to end.

Round 13: Sm, *C6B, p1, k2tog, k3, p1; repeat from * to end.

Round 14: Sm, *k6, p1, k4, p1; repeat from * to end.

Round 15: Sm, *k2tog, k4, p1, C4F, p1; repeat from * to end.

Round 16: Sm, *k2tog, k3, p1, k4, p1; repeat from * to end.

Round 17: Sm, *C4F, p1, k4, p1; repeat from * to end.

Round 18: Sm, *k4, p1, k4, p1; repeat from * to end.

Round 19: Sm, *k2tog, k2tog, p1, k2tog, k2tog, p1; repeat from * to end.

Round 20: Sm, *k2tog, p1, k2tog, p1; repeat from * to end.

You should have 36 (40, 44) sts on needles.

Next 2 rounds: Ssk to end [9 (10, 11) sts remain].

Cut yarn leaving a good tail and thread through the remaining stitches twice. Pull through and fasten securely on the WS of the beanie (inside).

FINISHING

Weave in all yarn ends and block the beanie using your preferred method.

CHARTS

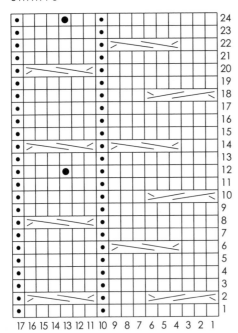

CROWN DECREASES

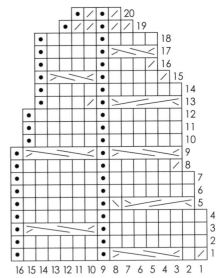

⟩⟨ C6B	☐ knit	⟋ k2tog	⟩⟨ C4F
⟩⟨ C6F	• purl	⟍ ssk	● make bobble (see Glossary)

WILD

The Sun is up. I can sense that way before I even wake up. Behind the flowery curtains the light is teasing me. Wake up, I'm here. Open your eyes. Come and play.

Opening the door leads me to everything green. I know the grass is getting longer; you have told me that it should have been mown weeks ago. But I like to see the neatly-kept grass turning into wilderness. I know I'm the only one. Last time I cut it, you had to do it again the next day. You asked if I had run out of gas for the mower. I said I wanted to see all the daisies.

I'm halfway up the garden path. I sit for a little while to think. The sun is high and bright. Yet it's nothing compared to the sun over there, I know that's what you would say. But to me it's bright. It's summer sun. It takes me out of the ordinary and tells me that I can dream of being anything. Bees hum nearby, soon there will be crickets. Do you remember that car? The red one, that took us through the mountains and back?

I remember that stream of cold water running; we jump over it again and again. *Laughing and holding hands.* The water is icy and no wonder; it comes straight from a glacier. The wild is here just as much as it was there. It looks so different, but one thing is certain: the wild is unexpected and sometimes easy to miss. Wilderness grows and finds new paths even if we try to tame it.

I will keep my wild side alive by daydreaming and finding those joyous moments *from within.*

WILD

MODERN VINTAGE SWEATER

TRANSITIONS SHAWL

TRANSITIONS SHAWL

by Joji Locatelli

This triangular shawl, with its beautiful color transformation, represents my own transitions in life, especially this year.

It reminds me of the season's changes; it makes me dream of fragrant cherry blossoms and travels... it gives me hope.

It is simple. It lets the yarn take center stage. Its rhythmic repeats are soothing to the mind and the soul, if you're looking for comfort while going through your own transitions.

TRANSITIONS SHAWL

SIZES

ONE SIZE

Finished measurements: 76" [190 cm] wingspan and 33½" [84 cm] deep at deepest point.

MATERIALS

Yarn: 3 skeins of Sock/Fingering by Barnyard Knits (75% merino / 25% Nylon; 463 yds [423 m] / 100 g) or approx. 300 yds [275 m] of fingering weight yarn in Color 1 (sample shown in colorway Leaf), 250 yds [228 m] in Color 2 (sample shown in colorway Flowering Dogwood) and 300 yds [275 m] in Color 3 (Sample shown in colorway Renaissance).

Needles: US 6 [4 mm] needles.

Other: 16 stitch markers, tapestry needle, blocking pins or wires.

GAUGE

16 sts and 32 rows = 4" [10 cm] in Garter stitch on US 6 [4 mm] needles. *Before you measure, please take the time to wash and block your swatch in the same manner that you will wash and block your shawl.*

FINISHED MEASUREMENTS

76" [190 cm]

33½" [84 cm]

TRANSITIONS SHAWL

INSTRUCTIONS

GARTER TAB

With Color 1, CO 3 sts. Knit 6 rows.

Next row (RS): K3, pick up and knit 3 sts along the side of your little rectangle (1 st from every purl ridge). Pick up and knit 3 stitches from the CO edge. *You will have 9 sts.*

Or use your preferred method for creating a garter tab that will give you 9 stitches.

From now on, the first st of every row should be slipped KNITWISE.

Set-up row (WS): Sl1, k3, pm, p1, pm, k to end.

SET UP

Row 1 (RS): Sl1, k2, m1R, k1, m1R, sm, k1, sm, m1L, k1, m1L, k3. *13 sts.*

Row 2 (WS): Sl1, k to m, sm, p1, sm, k to end.

Row 3: Sl1, k2, m1R, pm, yo, s2kp, yo, pm, m1R, sm, k1, sm, m1L, pm, yo, s2kp, yo, pm, m1L, k3. *17 sts.*

Row 4: Sl1, k to central m, sm, p1, sm, k to end.

Row 5: Sl1, k2, m1R, k to m, sm, yo, s2kp, yo, sm, k to m, m1R, sm, k1, sm, m1L, k to m, sm, yo, s2kp, yo, sm, k to 3 sts from end, m1L, k3. *21 sts.*

Row 6: Sl1, k to central m, sm, p1, sm, k to end.

Repeat **Rows 5-6** 13 more times. *You should have 73 sts.*

SECTION 2

Row 1 (RS): Sl1, k2, m1R, pm, yo, s2kp, yo, pm, k to m, sm, yo, s2kp, yo, sm, k12, pm, yo, s2kp, yo, pm, m1R, sm, k1, sm, m1L, pm, yo, s2kp, yo, pm, k to m, sm, yo, s2kp, yo, sm, k12, pm, yo, s2kp, yo, pm, m1L, k3. *77 sts.*

Row 2 (WS): Sl1, k to central m, sm, p1, sm, k to end.

Row 3: Sl1, k2, m1R, [k to m, sm, yo, s2kp, yo, sm] 3 times, k to m, m1R, sm, k1, sm, m1L, [k to m, sm, yo, s2kp, yo, sm] 3 times, k to 3 sts from end, m1L, k3. *81 sts.*

Row 4: Sl1, k to central m, sm, p1, sm, k to end.

Repeat **Rows 3-4** 13 more times. *You should have 133 sts.*

SECTION 3

Row 1 (RS): Sl1, k2, m1R, k to m, [sm, yo, s2kp, yo, sm, k to m] 2 times, sm, yo, s2kp, yo, sm, k12, pm, yo, s2kp, yo, pm, m1R, sm, k1, sm, m1L, pm, yo, s2kp, yo, pm, [k to m, sm, yo, s2kp, yo, sm] 3 times, k to 3 sts from end, m1L, k3. *137 sts.*

Row 2: Sl1, k to central m, sm, p1, sm, k to end.

Row 3: Sl1, k2, m1R, [k to m, sm, yo, s2kp, yo, sm] 4 times, k to m, m1R, sm, k1, sm, m1L, [k to m, sm, yo, s2kp, yo, sm] 4 times, k to 3 sts from end, m1L, k3. *141 sts.*

Row 4: Sl1, k to central m, sm, p1, sm, k to end.

Repeat **Rows 3-4** 13 more times. *You should have 193 sts.*

Row 31 (RS): Sl1, k2, m1R, k to m, [sm, yo, s2kp, yo, sm, k to m] 3 times, sm, yo, s2kp, yo, sm, k12, pm, yo, s2kp, yo, pm, m1R, sm, k1, sm, m1L, pm, yo, s2kp, yo, pm, [k to m, sm, yo, s2kp, yo, sm] 4 times, k to 3 sts from end, m1L, k3.

Row 32: Sl1, k to central m, sm, p1, sm, k to end.

Row 33: Sl1, k2, m1R, [k to m, sm, yo, s2kp, yo, sm] 5 times, k to m, m1R, sm, k1, sm, m1L, [k to m, sm, yo, s2kp, yo, sm] 5 times, k to 3 sts from end, m1L, k3.

Row 34: Sl1, k to central m, sm, p1, sm, k to end.

Repeat **Rows 33-34** 5 more times and then **Row 33** once more.

Rows 46-47: Change to Color 2, work as for row 34 and 33.

Rows 48-49: Change to Color 1, work as for rows 34 and 33.

Repeat **Rows 46-49** twice more and then **Rows 46-48** once more. *253 sts.*

Row 61 (with Color 1): Sl1, k2, m1R, k to m, [sm, yo, s2kp, yo, sm, k to m] 4 times, sm, yo, s2kp, yo, sm, k12, pm, yo, s2kp, yo, pm, m1R, sm, k1, sm, m1L, pm, yo, s2kp, yo, pm, [k to m, sm, yo, s2kp, yo, sm] 5 times, k to 3 sts from end, m1L, k3.

Row 62: Change to Color 2. Sl1, k to central m, sm, p1, sm, k to end.

Row 63: Sl1, k2, m1R, [k to m, sm, yo, s2kp, yo, sm] 6 times, k to m, m1R, sm, k1, sm, m1L, [k to m, sm, yo, s2kp, yo, sm] 6 times, k to 3 sts from end, m1L, k3.

Row 64: Change to Color 1. Sl1, k to central m, sm, p1, sm, k to end.

Row 65: Work as for row 63.

Row 66: Change to Color 2. Work as for row 64. Break yarn Color 1. From now on continue only with Color 2.

Repeat **Rows 63-64** 12 more times (without changing colors). *313 sts.*

Row 91: Sl1, k2, m1R, k to m, [sm, yo, s2kp, yo, sm, k to m] 5 times, sm, yo, s2kp, yo, sm, k12, pm, yo, s2kp, yo, pm, m1R, sm, k1, sm, m1L, pm, yo, s2kp, yo, pm, [k to m, sm, yo, s2kp, yo, sm] 6 times, k to 3 sts from end, m1L, k3. *317 sts.*

Row 92: Change to Color 3. Sl1, k to central m, sm, p1, sm, k to end.

Row 93: Sl1, k2, m1R, [k to m, sm, yo, s2kp, yo, sm] 7 times, k to m, m1R, sm, k1, sm, m1L, [k to m, sm, yo, s2kp, yo, sm] 7 times, k to 3 sts from end, m1L, k3. *321 sts.*

Row 94: Change to Color 2. Sl1, k to central m, sm, p1, sm, k to end.

Row 95: Work as for row 93. *325 sts.*

Row 96: Change to Color 3. Work as for row 94.

Repeat **Rows 93-96** once and then **Rows 93-94** once more. *You should have 337 sts.*

LACE EDGING

Charted Instructions

Row 1: With Color 2. Sl1, k2, m1R, work row 1 of Chart to central marker (removing the previous markers), m1R, sm, k1, sm, m1L, work row 1 of Chart to 3 sts from end, m1L, k3.

Row 2: Change to Color 3. Sl1, k2, work foll row of Chart to central marker, sm, p1, sm, work foll row of Chart to 3 sts from end, k3.

Row 3: With Color 3. Sl1, k2, m1R, work foll row of Chart to central marker, m1R, sm, k1, sm, m1L, work foll row of Chart to 3 sts from end, m1L, k3.

Row 4: Change to Color 2 and work as for row 2.

Row 5: With Color 2, work as for row 3.

Rows 6-9: Same as rows 2-5.

Row 10: Change to Color 3 and work as for row 2.

Break yarn Color 2. From now on continue with Color 3 only.

Continue working in pattern (repeating **Rows 3-4** but without changing color) until you have completed all 36 rows of the Chart. *You should have 409 sts.*

Written Instructions

Row 1: With Color 2. Sl1, k2, m1R, (k5, k2tog, yo, k1, yo, ssk, k5) to central marker (removing the previous markers), m1R, sm, k1, sm, m1L, (k5, k2tog, yo, k1, yo, ssk, k5) to 3 sts from end, m1L, k3.

Row 2: Change to Color 3. Sl1, k3, (k5, p5, k5) to 1 st from central marker, k1, sm, p1, sm, k1, (k5, p5, k5) to 4 sts from end, k4.

Row 3: With Color 3. Sl1, k2, m1R, k1, (k4, k2tog, yo, k3, yo, ssk, k4) to 1 st from central m, k1, m1R, sm, k1, sm, m1L, k1, (k4, k2tog, yo, k3, yo, ssk, k4) to 4 sts from end, k1, m1L, k3.

Row 4: Change to Color 2. Sl1, k4, (k4, p7, k4) to 2 sts from central marker, k2, sm, p1, sm, k2, (k4, p7, k4) to 5 sts from end, k5.

Row 5: With Color 2, sl1, k2, m1R, k2, (k3, k2tog, yo, k2tog, yo, k1, yo, ssk, yo, ssk, k3) to 2 sts

from central m, k2, m1R, sm, k1, sm, m1L, k2, (k3, k2tog, yo, k2tog, yo, k1, yo, ssk, yo, ssk, k3) to 5 sts from end, k2, m1L, k3.

Row 6: Change to Color 3. Sl1, k5, (k3, p9, k3) to 3 sts from central marker, k3, sm, p1, sm, k3, (k3, p9, k3) to 6 sts from end, k6.

Row 7: With Color 3. Sl1, k2, m1R, k3 (k2, k2tog, yo, k2tog, yo, k3, yo, ssk, yo, ssk, k2) to 3 sts from central m, k3, m1R, sm, k1, sm, m1L, k3, (k2, k2tog, yo, k2tog, yo, k3, yo, ssk, yo, ssk, k2) to 6 sts from end, k3, m1L, k3.

Row 8: Change to Color 2. Sl1, k6, (k2, p11, k2) to 4 sts from central marker, k4, sm, p1, sm, k4, (k2, p11, k2) to 7 sts from end, k7.

Row 9: With Color 2. Sl1, k2, m1R, k4, [k1, (k2tog, yo) 3 times, k1, (yo, ssk) 3 times, k1] to 4 sts from central m, k4, m1R, sm, k1, sm, m1L, k4, [k1, (k2tog, yo) 3 times, k1, (yo, ssk) 3 times, k1] to 7 sts from end, k4, m1L, k3.

Row 10: Change to Color 3. Sl1, k7, (k1, p11, k1) to 5 sts from central marker, k5, sm, p1, sm, k5, (k1, p11, k1) to 8 sts from end, k8.

Break yarn Color 2. From now on continue with Color 3 only.

Row 11: Sl1, k2, m1R, k5, [(k2tog, yo) 3 times, k3, (yo, ssk) 3 times] to 5 sts from central m, k5, m1R, sm, k1, sm, m1L, k5, [(k2tog, yo) 3 times, k3, (yo, ssk) 3 times] to 8 sts from end, k5, m1L, k3.

Row 12: Sl1, k8, p to 6 sts from central marker, k6, sm, p1, sm, k6, p to 9 sts from end, k9.

Row 13: Sl1, k2, m1R, k1, yo, ssk, yo, ssk, k1, [k1, (k2tog, yo) 3 times, k1, (yo, ssk) 3 times, k1] to 6 sts from central m, k1, k2tog, yo, k2tog, yo, k1, m1R, sm, k1, sm, m1L, k1, yo, ssk, yo, ssk, k1, [k1, (k2tog, yo) 3 times, k1, (yo, ssk) 3 times, k1] to 9 sts from end m, k1, k2tog, yo, k2tog, yo, k1, m1L, k3.

Row 14 and all following WS rows: Sl1, k2, p to central marker, sm, p1, sm, p to 3 sts from end, k3.

Row 15: Sl1, k2, m1R, k1, (yo, ssk) 3 times,

[(k2tog, yo) 3 times, k3, (yo, ssk) 3 times]
to 7 sts from central m, (k2tog, yo) 3 times,
k1, m1R, sm, k1, sm, m1L, k1, (yo, ssk) 3
times, [(k2tog, yo) 3 times, k3, (yo, ssk) 3
times] to 10 sts from end, (k2tog, yo) 3
times, k1, m1L, k3.

Row 17: Sl1, k2, m1R, k1, (yo, ssk) 3 times,
k1, [k1, (k2tog, yo) 3 times, k1, (yo, ssk)
3 times, k1] to 8 sts from central m, k1,
(k2tog, yo) 3 times, k1, m1R, sm, k1, sm,
m1L, k1, (yo, ssk) 3 times, k1, [k1, (k2tog,
yo) 3 times, k1, (yo, ssk) 3 times, k1] to 11
sts from end, k1, (k2tog, yo) 3 times, k1,
m1L, k3.

Row 19: Sl1, k2, m1R, k3, (yo, ssk) 3 times,
[(k2tog, yo) 3 times, k3, (yo, ssk) 3 times]
to 9 sts from central m, (k2tog, yo) 3 times,
k3, m1R, sm, k1, sm, m1L, k3, (yo, ssk) 3
times, [(k2tog, yo) 3 times, k3, (yo, ssk) 3
times] to 12 sts from end, (k2tog, yo) 3
times, k3, m1L, k3.

Row 21: Sl1, k2, m1R, k2tog, yo, k1, (yo, ssk)
3 times, k1, [k1, (k2tog, yo) 3 times, k1, (yo,
ssk) 3 times, k1] to 10 sts from central m,
k1, (k2tog, yo) 3 times, k1, yo, ssk, m1L, sm,
k1, sm, m1R, k2tog, yo, k1, (yo, ssk) 3 times,
k1, [k1, (k2tog, yo) 3 times, k1, (yo, ssk) 3
times, k1] to 13 sts from end, k1, (k2tog,
yo) 3 times, k1, yo, ssk, m1L, k3.

Row 23: Sl1, k2, m1R, k2tog, yo, k3, (yo, ssk)
3 times, [(k2tog, yo) 3 times, k3, (yo, ssk) 3
times] to 11 sts from central m, (k2tog, yo)
3 times, k3, yo, ssk, m1R, sm, k1, sm, m1L,
k2tog, yo, k3, (yo, ssk) 3 times, [(k2tog, yo)
3 times, k3, (yo, ssk) 3 times] to 14 sts from
end, (k2tog, yo) 3 times, k3, yo, ssk, m1L,
k3.

Row 25: Sl1, k2, m1R, k2tog, yo, k2tog, yo,
k1, (yo, ssk) 3 times, k1, [k1, (k2tog, yo)
3 times, k1, (yo, ssk) 3 times, k1] to 12 sts
from central m, k1, (k2tog, yo) 3 times,
k1, yo, ssk, yo, ssk, m1R, sm, k1, sm, m1L,
k2tog, yo, k2tog, yo, k1, (yo, ssk) 3 times,
k1, [k1, (k2tog, yo) 3 times, k1, (yo, ssk) 3
times, k1] to 15 sts from end, k1, (k2tog,
yo) 3 times, k1, yo, ssk, yo, ssk, m1L, k3.

Row 27: Sl1, k2, m1R, k2tog, yo, k2tog, yo,
k3, (yo, ssk) 3 times, [(k2tog, yo) 3 times,
k3, (yo, ssk) 3 times] to 13 sts from central

m, (k2tog, yo) 3 times, k3, yo, ssk, yo, ssk,
m1R, sm, k1, sm, m1L, k2tog, yo, k2tog, yo,
k3, (yo, ssk) 3 times, [(k2tog, yo) 3 times, k3,
(yo, ssk) 3 times] to 16 sts from end, (k2tog,
yo) 3 times, k3, yo, ssk, yo, ssk, m1L, k3.

Row 29: Sl1, k2, m1R, (k2tog, yo) 3 times,
k1, (yo, ssk) 3 times, k1, [k1, (k2tog, yo)
3 times, k1, (yo, ssk) 3 times, k1] to 14 sts
from central m, k1, (k2tog, yo) 3 times,
k1, (yo, ssk) 3 times, m1R, sm, k1, sm, m1L,
(k2tog, yo) 3 times, k1, (yo, ssk) 3 times,
k1, [k1, (k2tog, yo) 3 times, k1, (yo, ssk) 3
times, k1] to 17 sts from end, k1, (k2tog,
yo) 3 times, k1, (yo, ssk) 3 times, m1L, k3.

Row 31: Sl1, k2, m1R, [(k2tog, yo) 3 times,
k3, (yo, ssk) 3 times] to central m, m1R, sm,
k1, sm, m1L, [(k2tog, yo) 3 times, k3, (yo,
ssk) 3 times] to 3 sts from end, m1L, k3.

Row 33: Sl1, k2, m1R, k1, [k1, (k2tog, yo)
3 times, k1, (yo, ssk) 3 times, k1] to 1 st
from central m, k1, m1R, sm, k1, sm, m1L,
k1, [k1, (k2tog, yo) 3 times, k1, (yo, ssk) 3
times, k1] to 4 sts from end, k1, m1L, k3.

Row 35: Sl1, k2, m1R, yo, ssk, [(k2tog, yo)
3 times, k3, (yo, ssk) 3 times] to 2 sts from
central m, k2tog, yo, m1R, sm, k1, sm,
m1L, yo, ssk, [(k2tog, yo) 3 times, k3, (yo,
ssk) 3 times] to 5 sts from end, k2tog, yo,
m1L, k3.

You should have 409 sts.

PICOT BIND OFF

*CO 2 sts using the knitted cast on, BO 7 sts.
Move the remaining st on the RN back to
the LN. Repeat from * until you use up all
your sts.

You may need to adjust slightly the
frequency of the picots if you want to have
a picot right in the center of the shawl.

FINISHING

Weave in ends and block shawl to finished
measurements.

LACE CHART

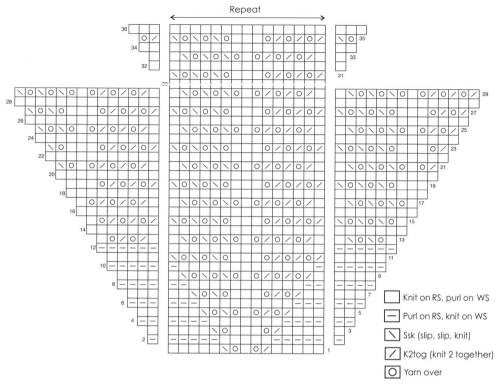

Knit on RS, purl on WS

— Purl on RS, knit on WS

\ Ssk (slip, slip, knit)

/ K2tog (knit 2 together)

O Yarn over

MODERN VINTAGE

by Veera Välimäki

Something so unknown, something so familiar; that's what makes the wild so intriguing, so tempting. There's something to relate to, there's something new to enjoy, and we are never quite sure of the outcome.

This sweater is the epitome of wild: we see the raglan shaping we are so used to, yet it's not quite the same. Worked in pieces with plenty of positive ease, this sweater takes us to our wild side and lets us play with color.

MODERN VINTAGE

SIZES

1 (2, 3, 4, 5, 6, 7, 8). Shown in size 3 on 38" bust.

Finished chest measurements: 40 (44, 48, 52, 56, 60, 64, 68)" [100 (110, 120, 130, 140, 150, 160, 170) cm]. Choose a size with approx. 8-12" [20-30 cm] ease. See schematics below.

MATERIALS

Yarn: 5 (5, 5, 5, 8, 8, 8, 8) skeins of La Bien Aimée X Mondim by Retrosaria Rosa Pomar and La Bien Aimée (100% non-SW Portuguese Wool; 421 yds [385 m] / 100 g); 3 (3, 3, 3, 4, 4, 4, 4) skeins in MC and 1 (1, 1, 1, 2, 2, 2, 2) skein(s) of each CC1 and CC2. Approx. 1700 (1800, 1950, 2080, 2200, 2320, 2460, 2600) yds [1550 (1650, 1780, 1900, 2010, 2120, 2250, 2380)] of fingering weight yarn; 980 (1040, 1160, 1250, 1320, 1400, 1500, 1600) yds [900 (950, 1060, 1140, 1210, 1280, 1370, 1460) m] in MC and 360 (380, 395, 415, 440, 460, 480, 500) yds [330 (350, 360, 380, 400, 420, 440, 460) m] in each CC1 and CC2. Sample knitted in colors Driftwood Graffiti (MC, speckled gray), Highgarden (CC1, pink) and Yellow Brick Road (CC2, yellow).

Needles: US 2½ [3 mm] and US 1½ [2.5 mm] circular needles, 32" [80 cm] long or longer.

Other: Tapestry needle and blocking aids.

GAUGE

24 sts and 30 rows = 4" [10 cm] in brioche ribbing, using larger needles. *Note: 30 rows back and forth are worked.*

24 sts and 30 rows = 4" [10 cm] in twisted ribbing, using smaller needles. *Before you measure, please take the time to wash and block your swatch in the same manner that you will wash and block your sweater.*

FINISHED MEASUREMENTS

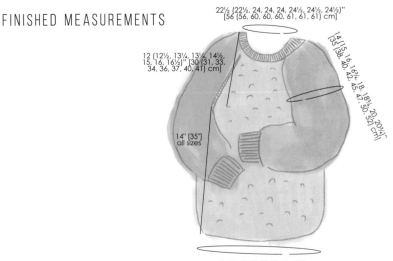

22½ (22½, 24, 24, 24, 24½, 24½, 24½)" [56 (56, 60, 60, 60, 61, 61, 61) cm]

12 (12½, 13¼, 13¼, 14½, 15, 16, 16½)" [30 (31, 33, 34, 36, 37, 40, 41) cm]

14 (15, 16, 16¾, 18, 18¾, 20, 20¾)" [35 (38, 40, 42, 45, 47, 50, 52) cm]

14" [35"] all sizes

40 (44, 48, 52, 56, 60, 64, 68)" [100 (110, 120, 130, 140, 150, 160, 170) cm]

MODERN VINTAGE

INSTRUCTIONS

SLEEVES

Note: Sleeves worked from shoulder to cuff.
Using the smaller needle and CC1, CO 33 sts (all sizes). Do not join. Work in twisted ribbing as follows –

Row 1 (RS): K5, *k1 tbl, p1; repeat from * to last 6 sts, k1 tbl, knit to end.

Row 2 (WS): K5, *p1 tbl, k1; repeat from * to last 6 sts, p1 tbl, knit to end.

Repeat **Rows 1-2** 10 more times.

Change to larger needle and begin brioche and increases as follows –

Setup Row (RS): K5, *k1, sl1yo; repeat from * to last 6 sts, k1, knit to end.

Setup Row (WS): K5, *sl1yo, brk1; repeat from * to last 6 sts, sl1yo, knit to end.

Row 3: K5, brkYObrk, sl1yo , *brk1, sl1yo; repeat from * to last 6 sts, brkYObrk, knit to end.

Row 4: K5, *sl1yo, brk1, repeat from * to last 6 sts, sl1yo, knit to end.

Rows 5, 7 and 9: K5, *brk1, sl1yo; repeat from * to last 6 sts, brk1, knit to end.

Rows 6, 8 and 10: K5, *sl1yo, brk1, repeat from * to last 6 sts, sl1yo, knit to end.

Repeat **Rows 3-10** 12 (13, 15, 16, 18, 19, 21, 22) more times. *You should have 85 (89, 97, 101, 109, 113, 121, 125) sts on needle.*

Continue in brioche and begin sleeve decreases as follows -

Rows 11, 13, 15, 17 and 19: K5, *brk1, sl1yo; repeat from * to last 6 sts, brk1, knit to end.

Rows 12, 14, 16, 18 and 20: K5, *sl1yo, k1, repeat from * to last 6 sts, sl1yo, knit to end.

Row 21: K5, bsk2p, sl1yo, *brk1, sl1yo;

repeat from * to last 8 sts, brk3tog, knit to end.

Row 22: K5, *sl1yo, brk1, repeat from * to last 6 sts, sl1yo, knit to end.

Repeat **Rows 11-22** 6 (6, 7, 7, 8, 8, 8) more times. Then repeat **Rows 11-12** until the sleeve measures 16" [40 cm] from the end of increases.

Change to smaller needle and work 12 rows in twisted ribbing as follows. *Note: Only on the first row of the twisted ribbing, work brk instead of 'k1 tbl'.*

Row 1 (RS): K5, *k1 tbl, p1; repeat from * to last 6 sts, k1 tbl, knit to end.

Row 2 (WS): K5, *p1 tbl, k1; repeat from * to last 6 sts, p1 tbl, knit to end.

BO all sts in twisted ribbing loosely on next RS row.

Make second sleeve similarly, but use CC2 instead of CC1.

BACK AND FRONT

Using the smaller needle and MC, CO 51 (51, 57, 57, 57, 59, 59, 59) sts. Do not join. Work ribbing as follows –

Row 1 (RS): K5, *k1 tbl, p1; repeat from * to last 6 sts, k1 tbl, knit to end.

Row 2 (WS): K5, *p1 tbl, k1; repeat from * to last 6 sts, p1 tbl, knit to end.

Repeat **Rows 1-2** 10 more times.

Change to larger needle and begin brioche and increases as follows –

Setup Row (RS): K5, *k1, sl1yo; repeat from * to last 6 sts, k1, knit to end.

Setup Row (WS): K5, *sl1yo, brk1; repeat from * to last 6 sts, sl1yo, knit to end.

Row 3: K5, brkYObrk, sl1yo, *brk1, sl1yo; repeat from * to last 6 sts, brkYObrk, knit to end.

Row 4: K5, *sl1yo, brk1, repeat from * to last 6 sts, sl1yo, knit to end.

Rows 5, 7 and 9: K5, *brk1, sl1yo; repeat from * to last 6 sts, brk1, knit to end.

Rows 6, 8 and 10: K5, *sl1yo, brk1, repeat from * to last 6 sts, sl1yo, knit to end.

Repeat **Rows 3-10** 7 (6, 8, 7, 8, 8, 9, 8) more times.

Then work increases on every 2ⁿᵈ RS row as follows –

Row 11: K5, brkYObrk, sl1yo , *brk1, sl1yo; repeat from * to last 6 sts, brkYObrk, knit to end.

Row 12: K5, *sl1yo, brk1, repeat from * to last 6 sts, sl1yo, knit to end.

Rows 13: K5, *brk1, sl1yo; repeat from * to last 6 sts, brk1, knit to end.

Rows 14: K5, *sl1yo, brk1, repeat from * to last 6 sts, sl1yo, knit to end.

Repeat **Rows 11-14** 8 (12, 12, 16, 18, 20, 22, 26) more times. *You should have 119 (131, 145, 157, 169, 179, 191, 203) sts on needle.*

Continue even in brioche as follows -

Rows 15: K5, *brk1, sl1yo; repeat from * to last 6 sts, brk1, knit to end.

Rows 16: K5, *sl1yo, brk1, repeat from * to last 6 sts, sl1yo, knit to end.

Repeat **Rows 15-16** until the body measures 13½" [33 cm] from the end of increases.

Change to smaller needle and work 12 rows in twisted ribbing as follows. *Note: Only on the first row of the twisted ribbing, work brk instead of 'k1 tbl'.*

Row 1 (RS): K5, *k1 tbl, p1; repeat from * to last 6 sts, k1 tbl, knit to end.

Row 2 (WS): K5, *p1 tbl, k1; repeat from * to last 6 sts, p1 tbl, knit to end.

BO all sts in twisted ribbing loosely on next RS row. Work the back piece similarly, also in MC.

FINISHING

Weave in all yarn ends carefully. Block all pieces to measurements using your preferred method. Seam pieces together using matress stitch (see Glossary), starting with raglan seams and continuing to sides of the body and lastly seaming the sleeves.

NATURAL

Hiking up a trail, feeling the path under my feet, forming and changing, *this is my happy place.* These trees, these stones, these flowers are my everyday trail. I know when to hop over a rock; I know when to stoop lower to avoid the low hedges. Every morning I start my day by walking this same route and every morning I watch the same views, yet they are never quite the same. The nature is constantly on the move, it's ever-changing.

Will nature change when I climb this little hill, when I become part of it? I always want to be a part of my surroundings, to take it all in. But can I stand here in the woods while the forest stays the same? The mystery is always there with me. I take a few more steps, up, up the hill and then I see the lake, miles after miles my eyes wander on the water – and I'm happy. There's something about seeing into that long distance that always calms me.

Being surrounded by nature always gives me hope. I am a part of this and I belong here. Nature connects us all. The sun will rise and set again, the changes of seasons are never-ending. I am part of something bigger and I am never alone.

The lake. Here I am again, down by the shore, hopping from rock to rock, trying not to slip. This is my favorite game. I know the water is freezing, but part of me just wants to jump in and feel the icy coldness on every bone. The other side just wants to keep everything as it is, dry and warm. I take my shoes off and dip my toes into the water. Like electricity, the cold creeps up the back of my neck. *I feel alive and I feel I belong here.*

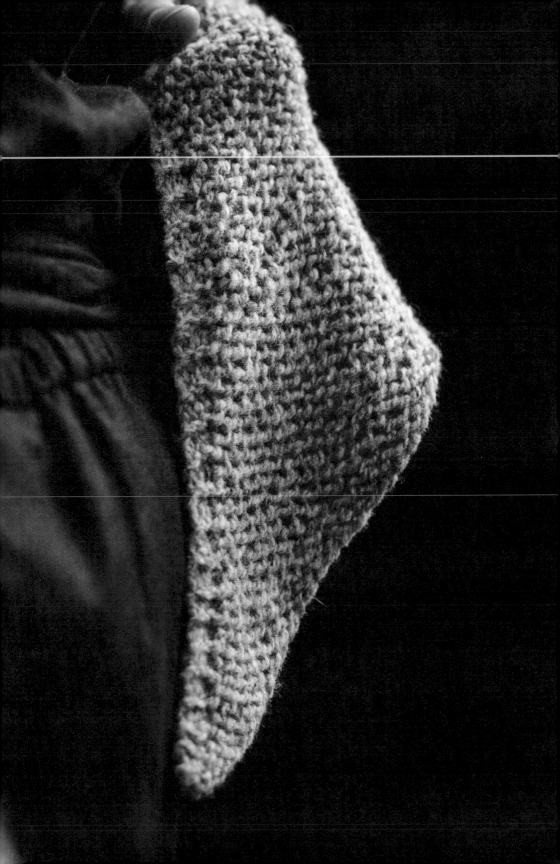

NATURAL

CHANGING PATHS SWEATER

SILVER ECHO SHAWL

CHANGING PATHS

by Joji Locatelli

I used to think, when I was younger, that one day I would see the path that I needed to follow in life. The path to security, steadiness, and happiness. I thought that once I saw it, all I had to do was stay on that trail, and as long as I followed it, everything would be as it should.

As I mature, I realize I cannot find happiness in stillness. Life is not a simple path that you must follow to have everything you desire. I must constantly seek branches from the path in order to find it.

Changing Paths is a top-down seamless sweater, with a modified saddle shoulder/raglan sleeve and a deep yoke. It is worked with 2 yarns held together: a Merino DK and a lace-weight mohair The body is simple stockinette stitch, but the sleeves are adorned with a changing path of eyelets, a simple lace pattern that will perhaps help you meditate on your path in life.

CHANGING PATHS

SIZES

1 (2, 3, 4, 5, 6, 7, 8, 9). Shown in size 3 on a 36" bust.

Finished bust circumference: 33¾ (37¼, 40¾, 44½, 48, 52½, 56¾, 60½, 65¾)" [84.5 (93.5, 102, 111, 120, 131, 142, 151, 164.5) cm]. Recommended ease: 2-4" [5-10 cm] of positive ease. See schematics below or more finished measurements at the end of the pattern.

MATERIALS

Yarn: 5 (5, 5, 6, 6, 7, 7, 8, 8) skeins of DK twist by Madelinetosh (100% merino; 250 yds [229 m] / 100 g) or approx. 1075 (1150, 1225, 1375, 1500, 1600, 1700, 1850, 1950) yds [984 (1053, 1122, 1259, 1374, 1465, 1557, 1694, 1786) m] of DK weight yarn (sample shown in colorway Kenobi).

4 (4, 4, 5, 5, 5, 6, 6, 6) skeins of Silk Cloud by Shibui Knits (60% kid mohair / 40% silk; 330 yds [300 m] / 25 g) or approx. 1075 (1150, 1225, 1375, 1500, 1600, 1700, 1850, 1950) yds [984 (1053, 1122, 1259, 1374, 1465, 1557, 1694, 1786) m] of lace-weight mohair yarn (sample shown in colorway Bone).

Both yarns are held together throughout the project.

Needles: US 8 [5 mm] and US 6 [4 mm] circular needles, about 32" long.

Other: Stitch markers, stitch holders or waste yarn, tapestry needle.

GAUGE

18 sts and 24 rows = 4" [10 cm] in Stockinette stitch on US 8 [5 mm] needles. *Before you measure, please take the time to wash and block your swatch in the same manner that you will wash and block your sweater.*

FINISHED MEASUREMENTS

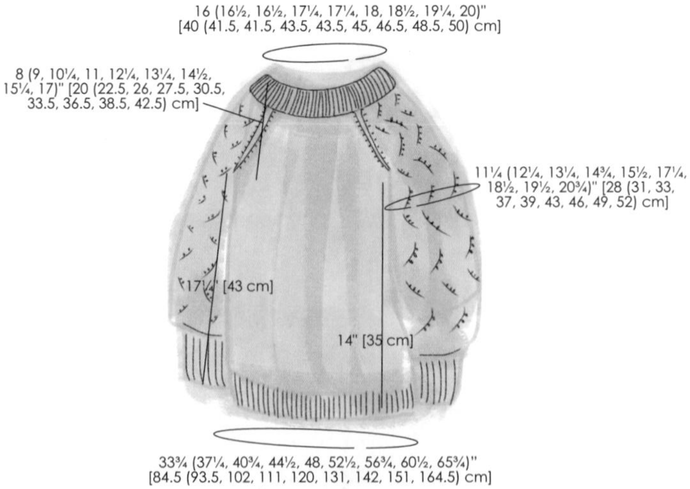

16 (16½, 16½, 17¼, 17¼, 18, 18½, 19¼, 20)" [40 (41.5, 41.5, 43.5, 43.5, 45, 46.5, 48.5, 50) cm]
8 (9, 10¼, 11, 12¼, 13¼, 14½, 15¼, 17)" [20 (22.5, 26, 27.5, 30.5, 33.5, 36.5, 38.5, 42.5) cm]
11¼ (12¼, 13¼, 14¾, 15½, 17¼, 18½, 19½, 20¾)" [28 (31, 33, 37, 39, 43, 46, 49, 52) cm]
17¼" [43 cm]
14" [35 cm]
33¾ (37¼, 40¾, 44½, 48, 52½, 56¾, 60½, 65¾)" [84.5 (93.5, 102, 111, 120, 131, 142, 151, 164.5) cm]

CHANGING PATHS

STITCHES USED

Path Lace (worked over 18 sts)

Find the chart on page 85.

Row 1: K to end.

Row 2 and all even-numbered rows: K to end if worked in the round, p to end if worked flat.

Row 3: (K6, k2tog, k1, yo) twice.

Row 5: (K5, k2tog, k1, yo, k1) twice.

Row 7: (K4, k2tog, k1, yo, k2) twice.

Row 9: (K3, k2tog, k1, yo, k3) twice.

Row 11: K to end.

Row 13: (Yo, k1, ssk, k6) twice.

Row 15: (K1, yo, k1, ssk, k5) twice.

Row 17: (K2, yo, k1, ssk, k4) twice.

Row 19: (K3, yo, k1, ssk, k3) twice.

Repeat **Rows 1-20** for pattern.

INSTRUCTIONS

NECKLINE

Using US 6 [4 mm] needles, CO 96 (100, 100, 104, 104, 108, 112, 116, 120) sts. Place marker and join for working in the round, being careful not to twist your stitches.

Work 10 rounds in k1, p1 ribbing.

Transfer your stitches to US 8 [5 mm] needles.

On the following section you will be working back and forth using short rows to shape the back neck.

Row 1: K4, wrap next st and turn (W&T - see Glossary).

Row 2: P4, sm, p24, pm, p24 (26, 26, 28, 28, 30, 32, 34, 36), pm, p24, pm, p4, W&T.

Row 3: K1, m1R, k2tog, yo, k1, sm, k1, yo, ssk, pm, work Path Lace, pm, k2tog, yo,

k1, sm, k1, yo, ssk, m1L , k to 3 sts before m, m1R, k2tog, yo, k1, sm, k1, yo, ssk, pm, work Path Lace, pm, k2tog, yo, k1, sm, k1, yo, ssk, m1L , k1, knit next st with wrap, W&T.

100 (104, 104, 108, 108, 112, 116, 120, 124) sts on the needles.

Row 4: P to last wrapped st and purl it tog with wrap, W&T.

Row 5: K to 3 sts from m, m1R, k2tog, yo, k1, sm, k1, yo, ssk, sm, work Path Lace, sm, k2tog, yo, k1, sm, k1, yo, ssk, m1L , k to 3 sts from m, m1R, k2tog, yo, k1, sm, k1, yo, ssk, sm, work Path Lace, sm, k2tog, yo, k1, sm, k1, yo, ssk, m1L , k to last wrapped st and knit it with wrap, W&T.

104 (108, 108, 112, 112, 116, 120, 124, 128) sts on the needles.

Row 6: P to last wrapped st and purl it tog with wrap, W&T.

Row 7: K to 3 sts from m, m1R, k2tog, yo, k1, sm, k1, yo, ssk, m1L , sm, work Path Lace, sm, m1R, k2tog, yo, k1, sm, k1, yo, ssk, m1L , k to 3 sts from m, m1R, k2tog, yo, k1, sm, k1, yo, ssk, m1L , sm, work Path Lace, sm, m1R, k2tog, yo, k1, sm, k1, yo, ssk, m1L , k to last wrapped st and knit it with wrap, W&T.

112 (116, 116, 120, 120, 124, 128, 132, 136) sts on the needles.

Row 8: P to last wrapped st and purl it tog with wrap, W&T.

Row 9: K to 3 sts from m, m1R, k2tog, yo, k1, sm, k1, yo, ssk, k to m, sm, work Path Lace, sm, k to 3 sts from m, k2tog, yo, k1, sm, k1, yo, ssk, m1L , k to 3 sts from m, m1R, k2tog, yo, k1, sm, k1, yo, ssk, k to m, sm, work Path Lace, sm, k to 3 sts from m, k2tog, yo, k1, sm, k1, yo, ssk, m1L , k to last wrapped st and knit it with wrap, W&T.

116 (120, 120, 124, 124, 128, 132, 136, 140) sts on the needles

Row 10: P to last wrapped st and purl it tog with wrap, W&T.

Row 11: K to 3 sts from m, m1R, k2tog, yo, k1, sm, k1, yo, ssk, k to m, sm, work Path Lace, sm, k to 3 sts from m, k2tog, yo. k1, sm, k1, yo, ssk, m1L , k to 3 sts from m, m1R, k2tog, yo, k1, sm, k1, yo, ssk, k to m, sm, work Path Lace, sm, k to 3 sts from m, k2tog, yo, k1, sm, k1, yo, ssk, m1L , k to last wrapped st and knit it with wrap, knit to the last wrapped st from the other side and knit it with wrap, completing the round.

120 (124, 124, 128, 128, 132, 136, 140, 144) sts on the needles; 34 (36, 36, 38, 38, 40, 42, 44, 46) sts for the front, 26 sts for the sleeves.

Place a marker at this point. This will be your new BOR.

Round 12: K to end of round.

YOKE SECTION 1

Round 1: K to 3 sts from m, m1R, k2tog, yo, k1, sm, k1, yo, ssk, m1L , k to m, sm, work Path Lace, sm, k to 3 sts from m, m1R, k2tog, yo, k1, sm, k1, yo, ssk, m1L , k to 3 sts from m, m1R, k2tog, yo, k1, sm, k1, yo, ssk, m1L , k to m, sm, work Path Lace, sm, k to 3 sts from m, m1R, k2tog, yo, k1, sm, k1, yo, ssk, m1L , k end of round. 8 sts increased.

Rounds 2, 4, 6: K to end of round.

Rounds 3, 5: K to 3 sts from m, m1R, k2tog, yo, k1, sm, k1, yo, ssk, k to m, sm, work Path Lace, sm, k to 3 sts from m, k2tog, yo, k1, sm, k1, yo, ssk, m1L , k to 3 sts from m, m1R, k2tog, yo, k1, sm, k1, yo, ssk, k to m, sm, work Path Lace, sm, k to 3 sts from m, k2tog, yo, k1, sm, k1, yo, ssk, m1L , k to end of round. 4 sts increased.

136 (140, 140, 144, 144, 148, 152, 156, 160) sts on the needles.

Repeat **Rounds 1-6** 4 (4, 5, 5, 6, 6, 7, 7, 8) more times.

You should have 200 (204, 220, 224, 240, 244, 264, 268, 288) sts; 64 (66, 72, 74, 80, 82, 90, 92, 100) sts for the front and back, 36 (36, 38, 38, 40, 40, 42, 42, 44) sts for the sleeves.

YOKE SECTION 2

Round 1: K to 3 sts from m, m1R, k2tog, yo, k1, sm, k1, yo, ssk, m1L , k to m, sm, work Path Lace, sm, k to 3 sts from m, m1R, k2tog, yo, k1, sm, k1, yo, ssk, m1L , k to 3 sts

from m, m1R, k2tog, yo, k1, sm, k1, yo, ssk, m1L , k to m, sm, work Path Lace, sm, k to 3 sts from m, m1R, k2tog, yo, k1, sm, k1, yo, ssk, m1L , k end of round. 8 sts increased.

Round 2: K to end of round.

Repeat **Rounds 1-2** 3 (6, 7, 9, 10, 13, 14, 16, 18) more times.

You should have 232 (260, 284, 304, 328, 356, 384, 404, 440) sts; 72 (80, 88, 94, 102, 110, 120, 126, 138) sts for the front and back, 44 (50, 54, 58, 62, 68, 72, 76, 82) sts for the sleeves.

Next round: K to 3 sts from m, k2tog, yo, k1, sm, k1, yo, ssk, m1L , k to m, sm, work Path Lace, sm, k to 3 sts from m, m1R, k2tog, yo, k1, sm, k1, yo, ssk, k to 3 sts from m, k2tog, yo, k1, sm, k1, yo, ssk, m1L , k to m, sm, work Path Lace, sm, k to 3 sts from m, m1R, k2tog, yo, k1, sm, k1, yo, ssk, k end of round. 4 sts increased.

You should have 234 (262, 286, 306, 330, 358, 386, 406, 442) sts; 72 (80, 88, 94, 102, 110, 120, 126, 138) sts for the front and back, 46 (52, 56, 60, 64, 70, 74, 78, 84) sts for the sleeves.

DIVIDE FOR BODY AND SLEEVES

Next round: K to m, remove m, place the next 46 (52, 56, 60, 64, 70, 74, 78, 84) sts on hold using a length of waste yarn (make sure you also transfer the markers), remove next marker. Using backwards loop CO 2 (2, 2, 3, 3, 4, 4, 5, 5) sts, pm, CO 2 (2, 2, 3, 3, 4, 4, 5, 5) sts, k to next marker. Place the next 46 (52, 56, 60, 64, 70, 74, 78, 84) sts on hold, remove next marker. CO 4 (4, 4, 6, 6, 8, 8, 10, 10) sts, k to end of round. Remove the marker indicating the beginning of the round and knit to side marker. This will be your new beginning of the round.

You should have 152 (168, 184, 200, 216, 236, 256, 272, 296) sts for the body.

BODY

Work in Stockinette st in the round until the sweater measures 13" [32.5 cm] from the armhole or 1" [2.5 cm] less than your desired length.

Switch to US 6 [4 mm] needles.

Next round: (K1, p1) to end of round.

Work in 1x1 ribbing for 1" [2.5 cm] and on the foll round BO all sts in pattern.

SLEEVES

With US 8 [5 mm] needles and starting at the center armhole, pick up and knit 2 (2, 2, 3, 3, 4, 4, 5, 5) sts. Place the 46 (52, 56, 60, 64, 70, 74, 78, 84) held stitches of a sleeve onto the left needle, k to m, sm, work next row of Path Lace, sm, k to end of row. Pick up and knit 2 (2, 2, 3, 3, 4, 4, 5, 5) more sts, reaching the center of the armhole again. Place marker. *You should have 50 (56, 60, 66, 70, 78, 82, 88, 94) sts.*

Next round: K to m, sm, work next row of Path Lace, sm, k to end of round.

Work 12 rounds in the established pattern.

Next round (decrease round): K1, ssk, work in patt to 3 st from end, k2tog, k1.

Continue working in pattern repeating a decrease round every 18 (10, 12, 8, 6, 6, 5, 5, 4) rounds 3 (6, 5, 8, 10, 10, 12, 13, 16) more times. *You should have 42 (42, 48, 48, 48, 56, 56, 60, 60) sts.*

When sleeve measures 14½" [36 cm], or 3¼" [8 cm] less than your desired length, switch to US 6 [4 mm] needles and start cuff.

Next round: [K5 (5, 4, 4, 4, 5, 5, 4, 4), k2tog] to end. 36 (36, 40, 40, 40, 48, 48, 50, 50) sts left.

Next round: (K1, p1) to end of round.

Work in the established ribbing for 3¼" [8 cm] and on the foll round BO all sts in pattern.

FINISHING

Weave in ends and block garment to schematic measurements.

FINISHED MEASUREMENTS

Neck opening: 16 (16½, 16½, 17¼, 17¼, 18, 18½, 19¼, 20)" [40 (41.5, 41.5, 43.5, 43.5, 45, 46.5, 48.5, 50) cm].

Bust circumference: 33¾ (37¼, 40¾, 44½, 48, 52½, 56¾, 60½, 65¾)" [84.5 (93.5, 102, 111, 120, 131, 142, 151, 164.5) cm].

Yoke depth: 8 (9, 10¼, 11, 12¼, 13¼, 14½, 15¼, 17)" [20 (22.5, 26, 27.5, 30.5, 33.5, 36.5, 38.5, 42.5) cm].

Upper sleeve circumference: 11¼ (12¼, 13¼, 14¾, 15½, 17¼, 18½, 19½, 20¾)" [28 (31, 33, 37, 39, 43, 46, 49, 52) cm].

Sleeve length from underarm to cuff: 17¼" [43 cm].

Length from underarm to hem: 14" [35 cm].

LACE CHART

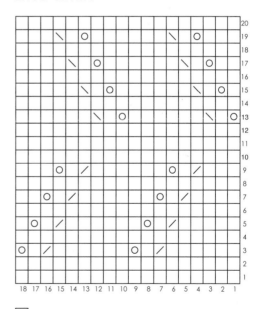

Knit on the RS, purl on the WS

O YO (Yarnover)

／ K2tog (knit 2 together)

＼ Ssk (slip, slip, knit)

SILVER ECHO

by Veera Välimäki

When I look at the soothing stitches moving on my needles, one by one, the shawl grows. That is the beauty of knitting: never-ending repetitions that make my heart full of joy. Silver Echo Shawl is built on those repetitions. Stitches move, they twist, and they change - yet the stitches always remain the same.

There's some garter stitch to soothe the wandering mind and some lovely twisted-stitch lace to help the mind focus. This simple triangle-shaped shawl lets the rustic light yarn shine. It's warm yet light, and will keep you company for many years to come.

SILVER ECHO

SIZES

ONE SIZE.

Finished measurements of the shawl: 85" [212 cm] wingspan and 36" [90 cm] deep.

MATERIALS

Yarn: 6 skeins of Shelter by Brooklyn Tweed (100% Wool; 140 yds [128 m] / 50 g). Approx. 820 yds [750 m] of worsted weight yarn. Sample knit in color Sweatshirt.

Needles: US 7 [4.5 mm] circular needles, 32" [80 cm] long or longer.

Other: Stitch marker, tapestry needle and blocking aids. Optional but recommended: Row counter.

GAUGE

16 sts and 28 rows = 4" [10 cm] in garter stitch on US 7 [4.5 mm] needles.

Before you measure, please take the time to wash and block your swatch in the same manner that you will wash and block your shawl.

FINISHED MEASUREMENTS

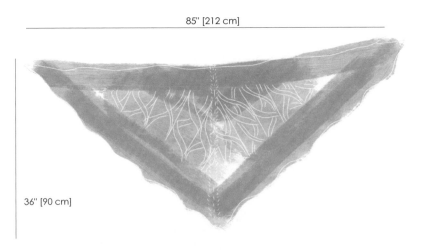

85" [212 cm]

36" [90 cm]

SILVER ECHO

INSTRUCTIONS

GARTER STITCH BEGINNING

Using the main needle, CO 7 sts. Do not join. Begin garter stitch.

Setup Row (RS): K1, k1fb, k1fb, pm, k1fb, k1fb, k2.

Setup Row (WS): Knit to end.

Row 1 (RS): K1, k1fb, knit to 1 st before marker, k1fb, sm, k1fb, knit to last 3 sts, k1fb, k2.

Row 2 (WS): Knit to end.

Repeat **Rows 1-2** 34 more times. *You should have 151 sts on needle.*

LACE

Begin lace. *Note: Find the lace charts at the end of the pattern.*

Row 3 (RS): K1, work row 1 of lace A to marker (working the repeat area a total of 6 times), sm, work row 1 of lace B to last 2 sts (working the repeat area a total of 6 times), k2.

Row 4 (WS): K2, work row 2 of lace B to marker, sm, work row 2 of lace A to last 2 sts, k2.

Row 5: K1, work the next row of lace A to marker, sm, work the next row of lace B to last 2 sts, k2.

Row 6: K2, work the next row of lace B to marker, sm, work the next row of lace A to last 2 sts, k2.

Repeat **Rows 5-6** 19 more times (all rows of lace worked once and then rows 1-18 of lace repeated once). *235 sts on needle.*

GARTER STITCH EDGING

Continue in garter stitch.

Row 7 (RS): K1, k1fb, knit to 1 st before marker, k1fb, sm, k1fb, knit to last 3 sts, k1fb, k2.

Row 8 (WS): Knit to end.

Repeat **Rows 7-8** 27 more times, or until you start to run out of yarn with enough to bind off. *You should have 347 sts on needle.* BO all sts loosely on next row (RS).

FINISHING

Weave in all yarn ends carefully. Block the shawl to measurements using wires and pins.

LACE CHARTS

LACE A

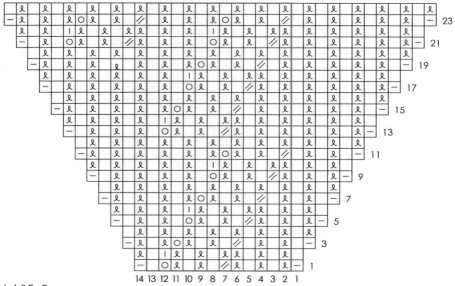

14 13 12 11 10 9 8 7 6 5 4 3 2 1

LACE B

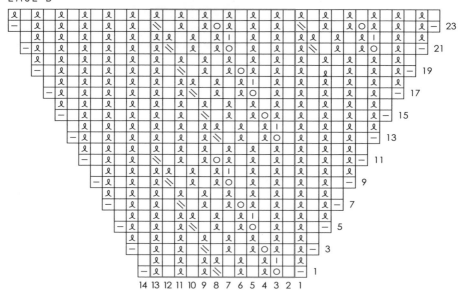

14 13 12 11 10 9 8 7 6 5 4 3 2 1

CHART KEY

ℓ Twisted St st: K1 tbl on RS, p1 tbl on WS	— K1fb
☐ Twisted rev St st: P1 tbl on RS, k1 tbl on WS	⧄ Slip one as if to p, k1, pass the slipped st over
Ⓞ Yarn over	⧅ K2tog tbl
⏐ Knit on RS	☐ Pattern repeat

BEYOND

Dare I dream of what's beyond today?

Dare I dream of all the things we will do? All the things we will discover and learn?

Yes, I do!

I close my eyes and I let my mind wander. I become a small, old car on a tiny, narrow road. There are slate mountains at each side, and I am going up, higher and higher. I can't see what's on the other side of the hill I am on, but I don't care! I'm going. All I may need is here with me: my sense of adventure and my wit. I just need to remember it.

I dream of going everywhere and taking you with me. Hold my hand; I know the way or you will find it. I am not scared anymore. In my dream, we can visit so many places and make so many wishes come true. In my dream, there will always be time, and it'll never be too late. In my dream, we will never be old.

I know it is hard sometimes to take the long road, the hard road, the unknown road. But the reward is the journey as well as the destination. Every challenge, every test we've overcome, is an obstacle we've weathered, and it's forever a memory together.

Grab your little suitcase of adventure and hop on. We have so much to talk about on the way!

BEYOND

OVERTHROW WRAP

SUNBEAM SWEATER

OVERTHROW WRAP

by Joji Locatelli

This triangular wrap was inspired by a leaf photograph I once found on the internet. I immediately knew I wanted to translate that into a shawl pattern, but I didn't know how exactly to achieve it. My designs often happen like that: in my mind there's an image of what my design must look like, but finding the right technique or strategy to get there is a challenge. Also, I always compare my design work with life.

When I was younger, these challenges were exciting. I had nothing to lose if I didn't get there, I had all to gain. I had my full creative life ahead of me and very few responsibilities. As I grow older, these challenges get harder to face, and I tend to avoid them...

Getting to the point, for the longest time I've avoided using brioche stitch in my patterns, or in my knitting, in general. For some reason I didn't understand it naturally (like I do with most other knitting techniques), so I avoided it. I could get away with telling myself I didn't really need it in my toolkit.

That changed when this leaf leaf occupied my mind. I could not escape from it. This design *had* to have brioche, I just knew it. I would have to face it and I was scared. Of what, you ask? Of failing. But wasn't I failing already by not trying? That's what I tell myself now that I've finally been able to use brioche for this pattern. I wish I could tell my younger self that failing was absolutely OK.

OVERTHROW WRAP

SIZES

ONE SIZE
Finished measurements: 72" [180 cm] wingspan. Depth at deepest point: 40" [100 cm].

MATERIALS

Yarn: 5 skeins of KidMohair Lace by Walk Collection (70% Mohair / 30% Silk; 460 yds [420 m] / 50 g). 1 skein in colors 1, 2, 3, 4 and 5; or approx. 184 yds [169 m] of lace-weight mohair yarn in Color 1 (sample shown in colorway Goldenrod); 276 yds [252 m] in Color 2 (sample shown in colorway Squirrel); 368 yds [336 m] in Color 3 (sample shown in colorway Apricot); 460 yds [420 m] in Color 4 (sample shown in colorway Arctic Fox); 368 yds [336 m] in Color 5 (sample shown in colorway Goiaba). *Notes: The mohair yarns are knit double stranded throughout the pattern. They can be substituted by a single strand of fingering weight yarn. You will need every single yard of Mohair color 4.*

1 skein of Cozy Merino by Walk Collection (100% Merino; 400yds [360 m] / 100g), or approx. 231 yds [211 m] of fingering weight yarn (sample shown in colorway Volcanic Sand). You will need two balls made up from this yarn (or you can knit from the inside and the outside of the ball when needed.

Needles: US 6 [4 mm] circular needles, 32" long.

Other: Stitch markers, tapestry needle.

GAUGE

17 sts and 34 rows = 4" [10 cm] in Garter stitch on US 6 [4 mm] needles, using 2 strands of mohair held together, before blocking.

FINISHED MEASUREMENTS

72" [180 cm]

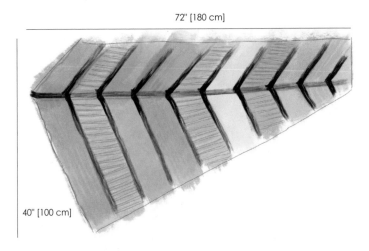

40" [100 cm]

OVERTHROW WRAP

INSTRUCTIONS

BEGINNING

With mohair 1 held double, CO 9 sts.

Set-up row (WS): Sl1, k1, k1fb, pm, move mohair forward, join contrast yarn (CC) and p3, move mohair backwards and continue working with it, pm, k1fb, k to end. *11 sts.*

Row 1 (RS): Sl1, k1, m1L, k to m, m1R, sm, k3 using CC (carry mohair along the back), sm, with mohair m1L, k to end. *14 sts.*

Row 2 (WS): Sl1, k to m, sm, p3 using CC (carry mohair along the front), sm, with mohair k to end.

Repeat **Rows 1-2** 13 more times. *You should have 53 sts (32 sts before 1st marker, 18 sts after second one).*

Row 29 (RS): Sl1, k1, k2tog, k to m, m1R, sm, k3 using CC (carry mohair along the back), sm, with mohair m1L, k to end. *54 sts.*

Row 30 (WS): Sl1, k to m, sm, p3 using CC (carry mohair along the front), sm, with mohair k to end.

Repeat **Rows 29-30** 5 more times. *59 sts (32 sts before 1st marker, 24 sts after second one).*

BODY OF THE WRAP

CC Stripe 1

Carry mohair up the side while working this stripe.

Row 1 (RS): With a second strand of CC, k2, k2tog, k to m, m1R, sm, k3 using your original strand of CC (carry second strand along the back), sm, with second strand of CC m1L, k to end.

Row 2 (WS): Sl1, k to m, sm, p3 using original strand of CC (carry second strand along the front), sm, k to end.

Row 3: Sl1, k1, k2tog, p to m, m1R, sm, k3 using original strand of CC, sm, m1L, p to 2 sts from end, k2.

Row 4: Sl1, k to m, sm, p3 using original strand of CC, sm, k to end.

Break second strand of CC. *You should have 61 sts (32 sts before 1st marker, 26 sts after second one).*

Section 1 Stockinette stitch

Row 1: With mohair, sl1, k1, k2tog, k to m, m1R, sm, k3 using CC (carry mohair along the back), sm, with mohair m1L, k to end. *62 sts.*

Row 2: Sl1, k1, p to m, sm, p3 using CC (carry mohair along the front), sm, with mohair p to 2 sts from end, k2.

Repeat **Rows 1-2** 9 more times.

You should have 71 sts (32 sts before 1st marker, 36 sts after second one).

CC Stripe 2

Work as for stripe 1.

You should have 73 sts (32 sts before 1st marker, 38 sts after second one).

Section 2 Brioche stitch

For this section, you will work with mohair 1 and mohair 2, both colors double stranded, and you must also keep the central spine in CC. Slip all sts purlwise unless otherwise stated.

Set-up row 1A RS: With mohair 1, k2, (sl1yo, k1) to m, sm, k3 using CC, sm, (k1, sl1yo) to 2 sts from end, k2. Don't turn work. Slide all the sts to the other end of the needle and get ready to work a RS row again.

Set-up row 1B RS: With mohair 2, sl2, (brp1, sl1yo) to m, sm, sl3 (holding mohair in back), sm, bring yarn to front, (sl1yo, brp1) to 2 sts from m, sl 2 wyif. Turn work.

Set-up row 2A WS: With mohair 1, sl1, k1, (sl1yo, brp1) to m, sm, p3 with CC (carry mohair in the front), sm, (brp1, sl1yo) to 2

sts from end, k2. Don't turn work. Slide all the sts to the other end of the needle and get ready to work a WS row again.

Set-up row 2B WS: Mohair 2, sl2, (brk1, sl1yo) to m, sm, slip 3 sts wyif, sm, (sl1yo, brk1) to 2 sts from end, slip 2 wyib. Turn work.

Row 1A (RS - Mohair 1): Sl1, k1, sl1yo, Brk3tog, (sl1yo, brk1) to 2 sts from m, sl1yo, BrkYObrk, sm, k3 using CC, sm, BrkYObrk, sl1yo, (brk1, sl1yo) to 2 sts from end, k2. Don't turn work. Slide the sts to the other end of the needle. Get ready to start a RS row again.

Row 1B (RS - Mohair 2): Sl2, (brp1, sl1yo) to 2 sts from m, p1, sl1yo, sm, sl3 (holding mohair in back), sm, bring yarn to front, sl1yo, p1, (sl1yo, brp1) to 2 sts from end, sl2 wyif. Turn work.

Row 2A (WS - Mohair 1): Sl1, k1, (sl1yo, brp1) to m, sm, p3 with CC (carry mohair in the front), sm, (brp1, sl1yo) to 2 sts from end, k2. Don't turn work. Slide all the sts to the other end of the needle and get ready to work a WS row again.

Row 2B (WS- Mohair 2): Sl2, (brk1, sl1yo) to m), sm, slip 3 sts wyif, sm, (sl1yo, brk1) to 2 sts from end, slip 2 wyib (leave yarn in back). Turn work.

Row 3A (RS- Mohair 1): Sl1, k1, (sl1yo, brk1) to m, sm, k3 using CC, sm, (brk1, sl1yo) to 2 sts from end, k2. Don't turn work. Slide all the sts to the other end of the needle and get ready to work a RS row again.

Row 3B (RS- Mohair 2): Sl2, (brp1, sl1yo) to m, sm, sl3 (holding mohair in back), sm, bring yarn to front, (sl1yo, brp1) to 2 sts from end, sl2 wyif. Turn work.

Row 4A: Same as Row 2A.

Row 4B: Same as row 2B.

At the end of this repeat you should have 75 sts (32 sts before 1st marker, 40 sts after second one).

Work 2 more repeats of **Rows 1-4**.

You should have 79 sts (32 sts before 1st marker, 44 sts after second one).

CC Stripe 3

Break mohair Color 1, carry mohair Color 2 up the side.

> **Row 1 (RS):** With a second strand of CC, k2, (knit the next purl stitch, the next knit st and the yarn-over attached to it together), (k1, brk1) to m, m1R, sm, k3 using original strand of CC, sm, with second strand of CC m1L, (k1, brk1) to 2 sts from end, k to end. Turn work.

> **Row 2 (WS):** Sl1, k to m, sm, p3 using original strand of CC, sm, with second strand of CC k to end.

> **Row 3:** Sl1, k1, k2tog, p to m, m1R, sm, k3 using original strand of CC, sm, m1L, p to 2 sts from end, k2.

> **Row 4:** Sl1, k to m, sm, p3 using your original strand of CC, sm, k to end.

Break the second strand of CC.

You should have 81 sts (32 sts before 1st marker, 46 sts after second one).

Section 3 Garter stitch

With Color 2.

> **Row 1 (RS):** Sl1, k1, k2tog, k to m, m1R, sm, k3 using CC (carry mohair along the back), sm, with mohair m1L, k to end.

> **Row 2 (WS):** Sl1, k to m, sm, p3 using CC (carry mohair along the front), sm, with mohair k to end.

Repeat **Rows 1-2** 13 more times.

You should have 95 sts (32 sts before 1st marker, 60 sts after second one).

The remainder of the shawl is a repetition of the sections above. The only difference is that you'll be using different colors. On the first repeat replace 'Color 1' with 'Color 2' and replace 'Color 2' with 'Color 3'.

On the following repeat replace the colors with the following ones.

Continue repeating these sections until you finish Section 3 (Garter stitch) using Color 5.

You should have a total of 203 sts.

> **Next row:** bind off all stitches using an elastic bind off.

FINISHING

Weave in ends and block shawl to finished measurements.

SUNBEAM SWEATER

by Veera Välimäki

Like a ray of light, a beam of sunshine, I love all things radiant. I simply adore the early morning light that comes through my bedroom window and makes me smile, just like I love the scorching midday rays on the beach. In the Sunbeam Sweater the light is captured in the colors and in the bold, modular colorwork.

This sweater is a new take on the circular yoke sweater, unusual in its short rows and modular knitting. It's worked in one piece from top down and has lots of ease for a swingy shape.

SUNBEAM SWEATER

SIZES

1 (2, 3, 4, 5, 6, 7, 8). Shown in size 3 on 38" bust.

Finished chest circumference: 40 (44, 48, 52, 56, 60, 64, 68)" [100 (110, 120, 130, 140, 150, 160, 170) cm]. Choose a size with approx. 8-12" [20-30 cm] positive ease. See schematics below.

MATERIALS

Yarn: 4 (4, 4, 5, 5, 5, 6, 6) skeins of Silky Singles by Suburban Stitcher (70% SW Merino, 30% Silk; 438 yds [400 m] / 100 g); 1 skein in each MC, CC1 and CC2 (*all sizes*) and 1 (1, 1, 2, 2, 2, 3, 3) skein(s) CC3. Approx. 1180 (1280, 1400, 1540, 1690, 1860, 2100, 2230) yds [1080 (1170, 1280, 1410, 1550, 1700, 1920, 2040) m] of fingering weight yarn; 320 (320, 320, 360, 360, 410, 410, 410) yds [290 (290, 290, 330, 330, 375, 375, 375) m] in MC, 240 (240, 240, 300, 300, 380, 380, 380) yds [220 (220, 220, 275, 275, 350, 350, 350) m] in CC1, 340 (380, 415, 415, 430, 430, 430, 430) yds [310 (350, 380, 380, 390, 390, 390, 390) m] in CC2 and 320 (360, 425, 520, 610, 740, 890, 1010) yds [290 (310, 400, 445, 545, 625, 720) m] in CC3. Sample knitted in colors Predictability (MC, pink), Chicory (CC1, yellow), Jon Snow (CC2, variegated brown-gray) and Walnut (CC3, brown). *Note: You can also work the lower body and sleeves in one color only; then you will need 2 (2, 2, 3, 3, 3, 4, 4) skeins of the 3rd color and no 4th color.*

Needles: US 2½ [3 mm] and US 1½ [2.5 mm] circular needles, 32" [80 cm] long or longer, and dpns in each size for Sleeves.

Other: Stitch markers, one removable, and tapestry needle.

GAUGE

26 sts and 38 rows = 4" [10 cm] in Stockinette stitch on US 2½ [3 mm] needles. *Before you measure, please take the time to wash and block your swatch in the same manner that you will wash and block your sweater.*

FINISHED MEASUREMENTS

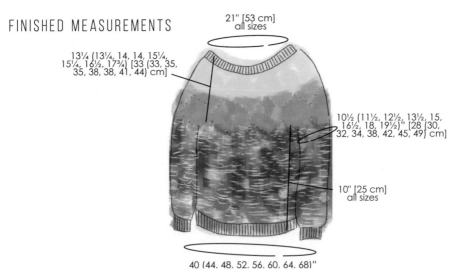

21" [53 cm]
all sizes

13¼ (13¼, 14, 14, 15¼, 15¼, 16½, 17¾) [33 (33, 35, 35, 38, 38, 41, 44) cm]

10½ (11½, 12½, 13½, 15, 16½, 18, 19½)" [28 (30, 32, 34, 38, 42, 45, 49) cm]

10" [25 cm]
all sizes

40 (44, 48, 52, 56, 60, 64, 68)"

SUNBEAM SWEATER

INSTRUCTIONS

COLLAR

Using the smaller needle and MC, CO 136 sts (all sizes). Carefully join in round without twisting your stitches and pm for BOR. Work 1½" [4 cm] in 1x1-ribbing [*k1, p1; repeat from * to end].

YOKE

Change to larger needle and work first set of increases: Sm, *k2, m1L; repeat from * to end. *You should have 204 sts on needle.* Begin short row shaping on next row:

Row 1 (RS): K30, W&T.

Row 2 (WS): Purl to m, sm, p30, W&T.

Row 3: Knit to m, sm, knit to previous wrapped st, pick up the wrap (k2tog the wrap with the wrapped st), k2, W&T.

Row 4: Purl to m, sm, purl to previous wrapped st, pick up the wrap (ssp the wrap together with the wrapped st), p2, W&T.

Repeat **Rows 3-4** 4 more times (all sizes). Knit to end of round.

Work 1" [2.5 cm] in St st. Work second set of increases on next round: Sm, *k3, m1L; repeat from * to end. *You should have 272 sts on needle.*

Work 1¼" [3 cm] in St st. Work third set of increases on next round: Sm, *knit 4 (4, 4, 4, 4, 2, 2, 2), m1L; repeat from * to end. *You should have 340 (340, 340, 340, 340, 408, 408, 408) sts on needle.*

Sizes – (-, -, 4, 5, 6, 7, 8) only: Work 1½" [4 cm] in St st. Work fourth set of increases on next round: Sm, *knit - (-, -, 5, 5, 3, 3, 3), m1L; repeat from * to end.

After all increases you should have 340 (340,

340, 408, 408, 544, 544, 544) sts on needle. Work in St st until the yoke measures 5 (5, 5, 6, 6, 6, 6, 6)" [12 (12, 12, 15, 15, 15, 15, 15) cm] from CO edge of the front.

SHORT ROW TRIANGLES IN MC

Continue with MC attached. Begin short row sets as follows. *Note: Each set of short rows uses 34 sts, keep the BOR marker in place.*

Short Row Set

Row 5 (RS): K2, W&T.

Row 6 (WS): Purl to end.

Row 7: Knit to previous wrapped st, pick up the wrap (k2tog the wrap with the wrapped st), k1, W&T.

Row 8: Purl to end.

Repeat **Rows 7-8** 14 more times. Move to start the next set: Knit to previous wrapped st, pick up the wrap (k2tog the wrap with the wrapped st), k1 (*Note: Now 34 sts are used from the yoke for this set of the short rows*). Place a removable stitch marker to indicate new starting point for the next set of short rows.

Continue repeating these Short Row Sets, starting with **Row 5** and working **Rows 7-8** 15 times as established, 9 (9, 9, 11, 11, 15, 15, 15) more times. Now all sts of the yoke are worked and you have reached BOR. Cut MC.

DIAMONDS IN CC1

Slide the last 34 sts worked back to left needle and turn work. Starting at the bottom corner point of the last short row triangle (MC) and using same larger needles, join CC1 to WS.

Setup Row (WS): Pick up and purl 34 sts.

Row 9 (RS): Knit 34, TW.

Row 10 (WS): Purl 33, p3tog (CC1 st together with 2 MC sts), TW.

Repeat **Rows 9-10** 14 times more, until you have used up all MC sts of that triangle edge.

Repeat from **Setup Row** 9 (9, 9, 11, 11, 15, 15, 15) more times, until all gaps are filled. Cut CC1.

SHORT ROW TRIANGLES IN CC2

Starting at BOR, the bottom corner point of the first short row diamond (MC) worked, and using same larger needles, join CC2 to RS.

Setup Row (RS): Pick up and knit 34 sts along the bottom edge of the CC1 diamond (to the next set of live CC1 sts on the needle), k2tog, W&T.

Setup Row (WS): P1, p2tog, W&T.

Row 11 (RS): Knit to previous wrapped stitch, k3tog the wrap with the wrapped st and the next st, W&T.

Row 12 (WS): Purl to previous wrapped stitch, p3tog the the wrap with the wrapped st and the next st, W&T.

Repeat **Rows 11-12** 14 times more, until 1 CC1 st of that diamond edge remains, on next RS row knit to previous wrapped stitch, k3tog the wrap with the wrapped st and the next st.

Repeat from **Setup Row** 9 (9, 9, 11, 11, 15, 15, 15) more times, until you reach BOR. Keep CC2 attached. Continue with CC2. Pick up the remaining wraps from the last short rows on first round: *Sssk the first st with the wrap and the wrapped st, k33; repeat from * to end. *Now you should again have 340 (340, 340, 408, 408, 544, 544, 544) sts on needle.*

Work in St st until the yoke measures 13¼ (13¼,14, 14, 15¼, 15¼, 16½, 17¾)" [33 (33, 35, 35, 38, 38, 41, 44) cm] from the front CO edge. Then divide for body and sleeves.

BODY

Dividing Round: Sm, knit 58 (60, 61, 72, 72, 90, 90, 91), place the next 54 (50, 48, 61, 60, 92, 91, 89) sts on holder for sleeve, CO 14 (23, 34, 26, 38, 15, 27, 38) sts using a backwards loop CO, knit 116 (120, 122, 142, 144, 180, 182, 184), place the next 54 (50, 48, 61, 60, 92, 91, 89) sts on holder for sleeve, CO 14 (23, 34, 26, 38, 15, 27, 38) sts using a backwards loop CO, knit to end.

You should have 54 (50, 48, 61, 60, 92, 91, 89) sts on each holder for the sleeves and 260 (286, 312, 338, 364, 390, 416, 442) sts on needles for the body.

Continue with CC2. Work in St st until you have approx. 15 (15, 18, 18, 20, 20, 22, 22, 24) grams of the CC2 yarn left (*Note: You will need some CC2 yarn for each sleeve, but try to use as much of the CC2 as possible*). Then fade to CC3 by working four 1 round stripes alternating with CC3 and CC2. Then cut CC2 and continue with CC3 alone.

Work in St st until the body measures 8" [20 cm] from underarm. Change to smaller needle and work 2" [5 cm] in 1x1-ribbing [*k1, p1; repeat from * to end]. BO all sts on next round in ribbing.

SLEEVES

Weigh the remaining CC2 and divide in 2 equal balls.

Join yarn to center of underarm CO sts and pick up and knit 7 (12, 17, 14, 19, 8, 14, 20) sts to sts on holder, knit 54 (50, 48, 61, 60, 92, 91, 89) st from holder, pick up and knit 7 (12, 17, 13, 19, 8, 13, 19) sts to center of underarm. *You should have 68 (74, 82, 88, 98, 108, 118, 128) sts on needles for sleeves.*

Work in St st until you have only a bit of the CC2 yarn left. Then fade to CC3 by working four 1 round stripes alternating with CC3 and CC2. Then cut CC2 and continue with CC3 alone.

When sleeve measures 2" [5 cm] from underarm, begin decreases.

Decrease Round: K2, k2tog, knit to last 4 sts, ssk, k2.

Repeat the **Decrease Round** 3 (3, 3, 4, 4, 5, 5, 5) more times on every 8th round. *60 (66, 74, 78, 88, 96, 106, 116) sts.*

Work in St st until the sleeve measures 11" [28 cm] from underarm. Change to smaller needle and work 2" [5 cm] in 1x1-ribbing [*k1, p1; repeat from * to end]. BO all sts on next round in ribbing.

FINISHING

Weave in all yarn ends carefully. Block the sweater to measurements using your preferred method.

LIGHT

It's time to open the window and let the *light inside*. Look around! It's so colorful now. It's all the things you imagined. It's all the things I wanted.

Light has tinted these images with the colors of autumn. Light made us smile. It made us beautiful and bright.

See how it peeks through the branches of that oak tree and how it dances on the agitated lake. See how it moves all around us and hugs us in a warm embrace. It was about time; we had been waiting for light for so long.

This light feels like a deep, deep breath of cool air filling our lungs. It makes our head feel... lighter, doesn't it?

I want to sit outside, under the sun and let its light take me in its arms. Please fill my body again with your energy. I'll bring my wool and needles and pretend *this light will stay with me forever.*

LIGHT

DUST AND CLAY SHAWL

AIMÉE CARDIGAN

AIMÉE CARDIGAN

by Joji Locatelli

This design is in honor of our friend Aimée. Always so chic, always so stylish, always finding the right colors.

This is a simple (or not so simple, as you'll discover) cardigan. Many could easily miss it among so many other designs. But the blocks of color, the combination of five spectacular colors, make it stand out. Make it so beautiful... extraordinary. Don't you already feel the urge to find in your stash five colors for this cardigan?

This is our friend Aimée's talent. We designers can do a fabulous job tailoring a design to perfection. But our work is always, always tied to yarns that we use. When we find the perfect yarn it's the beginning of a beautiful romance.

This cardigan has abundant ease, with perfectly tailored shoulders and set-in sleeves. It is worked seamlessly from the top down. The sleeves are picked up and worked in the round. The button-bands are worked once the cardigan is finished, to give the finished piece a professional look.

AIMÉE CARDIGAN

SIZES

1 (2, 3, 4, 5, 6, 7, 8, 9). Shown in size 3 on a 36" bust.

Finished chest circumference: 41¼ (45½, 50, 54½, 58¾, 62¾, 67¼, 72, 76)" [103 (114, 125, 136, 146, 157, 168, 180, 190) cm]. Recommended ease: 12-16" [30-40 cm] depending on how you like to wear your cardigans. See schematics below or more finished measurements at the end of the pattern.

MATERIALS

Yarn: 5 (5, 5, 10, 10, 10, 10, 10, 10) skeins of Merino Sport by La Bien Aimée (100% merino; 355 yds [325 m] / 100g). 1 (1, 1, 2, 2, 2, 2, 2, 2) skeins of each in 5 different colors, or approx. 1242 (1508, 1775, 2130, 2485, 2928, 3106, 3372, 3550) yds [1137 (1381, 1625, 1950, 2275, 2681, 2843, 3087, 3250) m] of light sport or fingering weight yarn; 248 (301, 355, 426, 497, 585, 621, 674, 710) yds [227 (276, 325, 390, 455, 536, 568, 617, 650) m] in each color. Sample shown in colorways: 1 Caramel (brown); 2 Maize (yellow); 3 Esmée (pink); 4 Artemisia (aqua green); 5 Emeline (dark green).

Needles: US 4 [3.5 mm] and US 3 [3.25 mm] circular needles, 32" long or longer, for the body and 40" for the button-band.

Other: Stitch markers, stitch holders or waste yarn, tapestry needle. 3 buttons of 5/8" [2 cm] diameter.

GAUGE

23 sts and 30 rows = 4" [10 cm] on US 4 [3.5 mm] needles in Stockinette stitch, worked flat.

24 sts and 30 rows = 4" [10 cm] on US 4 [3.5 mm] needles in Stockinette stitch, worked in the round, for the sleeves. *Before you measure, please take the time to wash and block your swatch in the same manner that you will wash and block your sweater.*

FINISHED MEASUREMENTS

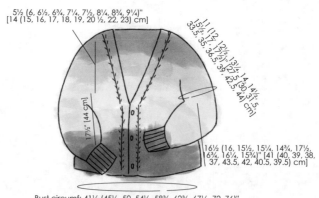

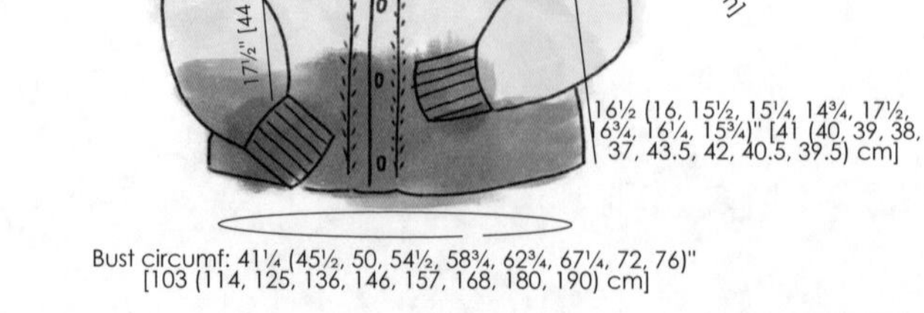
5½ (6, 6½, 6¾, 7¼, 7½, 8¼, 8¾, 9¼)"
[14 (15, 16, 17, 18, 19, 20 ½, 22, 23) cm]
11 (12, 12½, 13¼, 14, 14½, 15½, 17, 17½)" [27.5 (30, 31.5, 33.5, 35, 36.5, 39, 42.5, 44) cm]
17½" [44 cm]
16½ (16, 15½, 15¼, 14¾, 17½, 16¾, 16¼, 15¾)" [41 (40, 39, 38, 37, 43.5, 42, 40.5, 39.5) cm]
Bust circumf: 41¼ (45½, 50, 54½, 58¾, 62¾, 67¼, 72, 76)"
[103 (114, 125, 136, 146, 157, 168, 180, 190) cm]

AIMÉE CARDIGAN

INSTRUCTIONS

LEFT BACK SHOULDER

With Color 1 and using US 4 [3.5 mm] needles, CO 31 (34, 36, 37, 38, 40, 42, 44, 48) sts.

Row 1: K6, wrap next stitch and turn (W&T, see Glossary).

Row 2: P to end.

Row 3: CO 2, k to last wrapped st and knit it with wrap, k5 (5, 5, 5, 6, 6, 7, 7, 8), W&T.

Rows 4-5: same as rows 2-3.

Row 6: P to end.

Break yarn and put all sts on hold.

RIGHT BACK SHOULDER

CO 31 (34, 36, 37, 38, 40, 42, 44, 48) sts.

Row 1: K to end.

Row 2: P6, W&T.

Row 3: K to end.

Row 4: CO 2, p to last wrapped st and purl it with wrap, p5 (5, 5, 5, 6, 6, 7, 7, 8), W&T.

Rows 5 and 6: Same as rows 3 and 4.

JOIN BACK

Row 7: K to end of row. With cable cast on, CO 33 (35, 36, 36, 38, 40, 40, 41, 42) sts. Place the sts you had on hold for the other shoulder on the needles. K to last wrapped st and knit it with wrap, k5 (5, 5, 5, 6, 6, 7, 7, 8), W&T.

You should have 103 (111, 116, 118, 122, 128, 132, 137, 146) sts on the needles.

Row 8: P to last wrapped st and p it with wrap, p5 (5, 5, 5, 6, 6, 7, 7, 8), W&T.

Row 9: K to last wrapped st and knit it with wrap, k to end.

Row 10: P to last wrapped st and purl it with wrap, p to end.

ATTENTION, the following instructions must be worked at the same time:

Continue working straight in Stockinette st. When work measures 4½ (4½, 4½, 4½, 4½, 5, 5, 5, 5)" [11 (11, 11, 11, 11, 12.5, 12.5, 12.5, 12.5) cm] from the CO edge (measured along the sleeve edge), break yarn Color 1 and change to Color 2. Depending on the size you are making, this may happen before or after the armhole shaping starts.

Work straight until work measures 4¼ (3¼, 3½, 3½, 3¾, 4, 4, 4½, 4¾)" [10.5 (8.5, 9, 9, 9.5, 10, 10, 11.5, 12) cm] from CO edge. (It is correct that smallest size starts this shaping later)

Armhole shaping:

Row 1 (RS): K2, m1L, k to 2 sts from end, m1R, k2.

Row 2 (WS): P to end.

Repeat these 2 rows 3 (5, 9, 10, 11, 12, 14, 15, 17) more times.

Next row (RS): K2, m1L, k to 2 sts from end, m1R, k2.

Next row (WS): P2, m1R (purl), p to 2 sts from end, m1L (purl), p2.

You should have 115 (127, 140, 144, 150, 158, 166, 173, 186) sts on the needles.

Break yarn and put all sts on hold.

RIGHT FRONT

With US 4 [3.5 mm] needles, Color 1 and RS facing you, pick up and knit 31 (34, 36, 37, 38, 40, 42, 44, 48) sts along the right shoulder CO, starting at the sleeve edge and finishing at the neck edge.

Row 1 (WS): P5 (5, 5, 5, 6, 6, 7, 7, 8), W&T.

Row 2: K to end.

Row 3: P to last wrapped st and purl with wrap, p5 (5, 5, 5, 6, 6, 7, 7, 8), W&T.

Row 4: K to end.

Rows 5-6: Same as rows 3-4.

Row 7: Same as row 3.

Row 8 - neck increase row: K to 2 sts from end, m1R, k2.

Row 9: P to last wrapped st and purl it with wrap, p to end.

ATTENTION, the following instructions must be

worked at the same time:

Continue working in Stockinette stitch. Increase one stitch at neck edge (as indicated on row 8) every 6th following row twice more and then every 4th following row.

When work measures 4½ (4½, 4½, 4½, 4½, 5, 5, 5, 5)" [11 (11, 11, 11, 11, 12.5, 12.5, 12.5, 12.5) cm] from the CO edge (measured along the sleeve edge), break yarn Color 1 and change to Color 2. Depending on the size you are making, this may happen before or after the armhole shaping starts.

Continue working in this manner until work measures 4¼ (3¼, 3½, 3½, 3¾, 4, 4, 4½, 4¾)" [10.5 (8.5, 9, 9, 9.5, 10, 10, 11.5, 12) cm] from CO edge, measured along the armhole edge.

Armhole Shaping: (work the neck increases in this section too)

> **Row 1 (RS):** K2, m1L, work in patt to end.
> **Row 2 (WS):** P to end.

Repeat **Rows 1-2** 3 (5, 9, 10, 11, 12, 14, 15, 17) more times.

> **Next row (RS):** K2, m1L, work in patt to end.
> **Next row (WS):** P to 2 sts from end, m1L (purl), p2.

Break yarn and put all sts on hold.

LEFT FRONT

With US 4 [3.5mm] needles, Color 1 and RS facing you, pick up and knit 31 (34, 36, 37, 38, 40, 42, 44, 48) sts along the left shoulder CO, starting at the neck edge and ending at the sleeve edge.

> **Row 1 (WS):** P to end.
> **Row 2 (RS):** K5 (5, 5, 5, 6, 6, 7, 7, 8), W&T.
> **Row 3:** P to end.
> **Row 4:** K to last wrapped st and knit it with wrap, k5 (5, 5, 5, 6, 6, 7, 7, 8), W&T.
> **Rows 5-6:** Same as Rows 3-4.
> **Row 7:** P to end.
> **Row 8 - neck increase row:** K2, m1L, k to last wrapped st and knit it with wrap, k5 (5, 5, 5, 6, 6, 7, 7, 8), W&T.

> **Row 9:** P to end.
> **Row 10:** K to last wrapped st and knit it with wrap, k to end.

ATTENTION, the following instructions must be worked together:

Continue working in Stockinette stitch. Increase one stitch at neck edge (as indicated on row 8) every 6th following row twice more and then every 4th following row.

When work measures 4½ (4½, 4½, 4½, 4½, 5, 5, 5, 5)" [11 (11, 11, 11, 11, 12.5, 12.5, 12.5, 12.5 cm] from the CO edge (measured along the sleeve edge), break yarn Color 1 and change to Color 2. Depending on the size you are making, this may happen before or after the armhole shaping starts.

Continue working in this manner until work measures 4¼ (3¼, 3½, 3½, 3¾, 4, 4, 4½, 4¾)" [10.5 (8.5, 9, 9, 9.5, 10, 10, 11.5, 12) cm] from CO edge, measured along the armhole edge.

Armhole shaping: (work the neck increases in this section too)

> **Row 1 (RS):** Work in patt to 2 sts from end, m1R, k2.
> **Row 2 (WS):** P to end.

Repeat these 2 rows 3 (5, 9, 10, 11, 12, 14, 15, 17) times.

> **Next row: (RS):** Work in patt to 2 sts from end, m1R, k2.
> **Next row (WS):** P2, m1R (purl), p to end.

Don't break yarn.

JOIN BODY

> **Next row (RS):** Work in patt to end of row. CO 2 (2, 2, 6, 9, 12, 13, 14, 14) sts, place marker, CO 2 (2, 2, 6, 9, 12, 13, 14, 14) sts. Place the sts you had on hold for the back on the needles, k to end of row. CO 2 (2, 2, 6, 9, 12, 13, 14, 14), pm, CO 2 (2, 2, 6, 9, 13, 12, 14, 14). Place the sts you had on hold for the right front on the needles, work in patt to end.

You should have 119 (131, 144, 156, 168, 182, 192, 201, 214) sts for the back, and your stitch count for the fronts will depend on

how many neck increases you have worked.

When the band of Color 2 measures 4½ (4½, 4½, 4½, 4½, 5, 5, 5, 5)" [11 (11, 11, 11, 11, 12.5, 12.5, 12.5, 12.5) cm] break yarn and switch to Color 3, and then switch to Colors 4 and 5 when each band reaches the same length.

Continue working in Stockinette stitch and increasing at neck edge every 4 rows until you have 58 (64, 70, 76, 82, 89, 94, 98, 104) sts for each front.

AT THE SAME TIME, when work measures 4" [10 cm] from the underarm, work side increases as follows:

> **Side increase row:** Work in patt to 4 sts before marker, m1R, k4, sm, k4, m1L, k to 4 sts before next marker, m1R, k4, sm, k4, m1L, work in patt to end of row.

Repeat the side increase row every 20th following row.

Continue working in pattern until work measures approx. 14½ (14, 13½, 13¼, 12¾, 15¼, 14¾, 14¼, 13¾)" [36 (35, 34, 33, 32, 38.5, 37, 35.5, 34.5) cm] from the underarm or until the band of Color 5 measures 2½ (2½, 2½, 2½, 2½, 3, 3, 3, 3)" [5 (5, 5, 5, 5, 6, 6, 6, 6) cm]. Change to US 3 [3.25 mm] needles and work hem.

> **Next row (RS):** K1 (p1, k1) to end of row.
> **Next row (WS):** P1, (k1, p1) to end.

Continue working in the established ribbing until the hem measures 2" [5 cm]. BO all sts in pattern.

LEFT SLEEVE

With the RS facing you and US 4 [3.5 mm] needles, get ready to pick up stitches starting at the front armhole, at the line where Color 1 meets Color 2.

With Color 1, pick up and knit 24 (24, 24, 24, 24, 28, 28, 28, 28) sts from the front armhole, reaching the shoulder seam and then pick up 24 (24, 24, 24, 24, 28, 28, 28, 28) more sts from the back armhole, reaching the line where Color 2 begins. Break yarn.

With Color 2, and using the same needle, pick up and knit 9 (12, 14, 16, 18, 16, 19, 23,

25) sts from the back, reaching the centre of the armhole, place marker. Then pick up and knit 9 (12, 14, 16, 18, 16, 19, 23, 25) sts from the front, reaching the point where you started picking up sts again. *You should have 66 (72, 76, 80, 84, 88, 94, 102, 106) sts.*

Rejoin Color 1. You can leave Color 2 attached, hanging at the back of your work.

> **Row 1:** K35 (36, 37, 37, 38, 43, 44, 45, 46), W&T.
> **Row 2:** P22 (24, 26, 26, 28, 30, 32, 34, 36), W&T.
> **Row 3:** K to last wrapped st and knit it with wrap, k1, W&T.
> **Row 4:** P to last wrapped st and purl it with wrap, p1, W&T.

Repeat **Rows 3-4** twice.

> **Row 9:** K to last wrapped st and knit it with wrap, W&T.
> **Row 10:** P to last wrapped st and purl it with wrap, W&T.

Repeat **Rows 9-10** 5 (4, 3, 3, 2, 5, 4, 3, 2) more times.

You should have reached the point where Color 1 meets Color 2. Break yarn Color 1, pick up Color 2.

Continue to repeat **Rows 9-10** until 10 sts remain unworked at each side of the marker.

Work **Rows 3-4** 3 more times.

> **Next round:** K to last wrapped st and knit it with its wrap, k to end of round.
> **Next round:** K to end of round picking up last wrap when you find it.

Continue knitting in the round in Stockinette stitch.

IMPORTANT, switch to the next color every 4½ (4½, 4½, 4½, 4½, 5, 5, 5, 5)" [11 (11, 11, 11, 11, 12.5, 12.5, 12.5, 12.5) cm] as you did for the body. Make sure your first color change matches the color changes in your body.

At the same time, when work measures 2" [5 cm] from the armhole, start sleeve decreases.

> **Next round (decrease round):** K1, ssk, work in patt to 3 st from end, k2tog, k1.

Continue working in pattern repeating a decrease round every 14 (10, 10, 8, 7, 7, 5, 5, 4) rounds 6 (9, 9, 11, 13, 13, 16, 18, 20) more times.

You should have 52 (52, 56, 56, 56, 60, 60, 64, 64) sts.

When sleeve measures 14½" [36 cm], or 3¼" [8 cm] less than your desired length, switch to US 3 (3.25mm) needles and start cuff.

Next round: [K11 (11, 12, 12, 12, 13, 13, 14, 14), k2tog] to end. *You should have 48 (48, 52, 52, 52, 56, 56, 60, 60) sts left.*

Next round: (K1, p1) to end of round.

Work in the established ribbing for 3¼" [8 cm] and on the foll round BO all sts in pattern.

RIGHT SLEEVE

With the RS facing you and US 4 [3.5 mm] needles, get ready to pick up stitches starting at the back armhole, at the line where Color 1 meets Color 2.

With Color 1, pick up and knit 24 (24, 24, 24, 24, 28, 28, 28, 28) sts from the back armhole, reaching the shoulder seam and then pick up 24 (24, 24, 24, 24, 28, 28, 28, 28) more sts from the front armhole, reaching the line with Color 2. Break yarn.

With Color 2, and using the same needle, pick up and knit 9 (12, 14, 16, 18, 16, 19, 23, 25) sts from the front, reaching the centre of the armhole, place marker. Then pick up and knit 9 (12, 14, 16, 18, 16, 19, 23, 25) sts from the back, reaching the point where you started picking up sts again. *You should have 66 (72, 76, 80, 84, 88, 94, 102, 106) sts.*

Work the rest of the sleeve as you did for the left one.

BUTTONBANDS

The button-bands of this cardigan are worked afterwards in order to use a smaller needle that will give more structure to the bands. They are worked back and forth and attached to the main sweater at the end of every right side row.

Before starting, you will have to pick up

stitches along the entire front opening of the sweater, so make sure your needle is long enough (I recommend at least a 40" long needle).

Using your US 3 [3.25mm] needle PICK UP (do not knit) stitches along the opening of your cardigan. Start at the bottom corner of the right front, and pick up 1 st every 2 rows until you reach the back neck.

Once you get to the back neck section, you have to pick up 1 stitch for every stitch you have in the back neck. Pick up just one leg from each stitch until you reach the left front.

Now pick up stitches all the way down your left front: pick up 1 stitch for every 2 rows.

It is not important how many stitches you pick up, it's important that you keep this pick up ratio.

Once you've picked up all your stitches, you are ready to begin the button-band. You can use the same needle or a shorter, different one for this.

Pick up the end of the needle that is at the corner of your right front again. Using US 3 [3.25 mm] needles and Color 5, cable cast on 14 stitches by inserting the needle between the first and second stitches you picked up, and then continuing to cast on the rest of the stitches.

Row 1 (RS): K2, (p1, k1) 5 times, p1, ssk using one st from your button-band and 1 picked up stitch. Turn work.

Row 2 (WS): Sl1 with yarn in front, k1, (p1, k1) 5 times, slip 2 sts pwise with yarn in front. Turn work.

Repeat **Rows 1-2** 4 more times.

Buttonhole:

Row 1: K2, (p1, k1) 5 times, p1, ssk using one st from your button-band and 1 picked up stitch. Turn work.

Row 2 (WS): Sl1 with yarn in front, k1, (p1, k1) twice, turn work.

Row 3 (RS): (P1, k1) twice, p1, ssk using one st from your button-band and 1 picked up stitch. Turn work.

Rows 4-5: Repeat Rows 2-3.

Row 6: Sl1 with yarn in front, k1, (p1, k1) twice. Break yarn. Rejoin yarn to start working the remaining un-worked sts on the needle. (P1, k1) 3 times, sl 2 pwise. Turn work.

Row 7: K2, (p1, k1) 3 times. Turn work.

Row 8: (P1, k1) 3 times, sl 2 pwise. Turn work.

Rows 9-10: Repeat Rows 7-8.

After you finish **Rows 1-10** from the buttonhole, you can go back to repeating **Rows 1-2** from the main section of the button-band until you need to start another buttonhole.

In my sample, I only added 3 buttons, as I didn't plan to wear this cardigan buttoned down much and I didn't want to add any extra weight. You can use pins to mark the placement of your buttonholes after you've finished the first one and work as many as you like. In my sample they are spaced 4" [10 cm] apart.

Continue repeating **Rows 1-2** and change colors as your meet the transition with the next color block, always starting a new color on a RS row. Work your way around your cardigan opening. Bind off all stitches during the last joining row. Break yarn and fasten off.

FINISHING

Weave in ends and block cardigan. Sew buttons opposite to buttonholes.

FINISHED MEASUREMENTS

Bust circumference when worn closed: 41¼ (45½, 50, 54½, 58¾, 62¾, 67¼, 72, 76)" [103 (114, 125, 136, 146, 157, 168, 180, 190) cm].

Armhole depth: 5½ (6, 6½, 6¾, 7¼, 7½, 8¼, 8¾, 9¼)" [14 (15, 16, 17, 18, 19, 20 ½, 22, 23) cm].

Upper sleeve circumference: 11 (12, 12½, 13¼, 14, 14½, 15½, 17, 17½)" [27.5 (30, 31.5, 33.5, 35, 36.5, 39, 42.5, 44) cm].

Sleeve length from underarm to cuff: 17½" [44 cm].

Cardigan length from underarm to hem: 16½ (16, 15½, 15¼, 14¾, 17½, 16¾, 16¼, 15¾)" [41 (40, 39, 38, 37, 43.5, 42, 40.5, 39.5) cm].

DUST AND CLAY SHAWL

by Veera Välimäki

Soft summer air moves in every stitch of this featherweight shawl. Little bits of delicate lace worked in mohair look exactly like fireweed late in the summer, reminding us of those lovely days and never-ending sunshine.

The silk mohair is paired with some stripes and an easy-to-remember variation of feather and fan lace. The slightly asymmetrical crescent shape is lovely to wear.

DUST AND CLAY SHAWL

SIZES

ONE SIZE

Finished measurements of the shawl: 92" [234 cm] wingspan and 20" [51 cm] deep at deepest point.

MATERIALS

Yarn: 1 skein of Earth by Life in the Long Grass (70% SW Merino, 20% Yak, 10% Nylon; 438 yds [400 m] / 100 g) and 1 skein of Mohair Silk Lace by Life in the Long Grass (70% Kid Mohair, 30% Silk; 460 yds [420 m] / 50 g). Approx. 380 yds [410 m] of fingering weight yarn and 430 yds [400 m] of lace-weight yarn. Sample knit in colours Henna Rose (MC, Earth) and Agate Rose (CC, Mohair Silk Lace).

Needles: US 6 [4 mm] circular needles, 32" [80 cm] long or longer.

Other: Stitch markers, tapestry needle, spare yarn for provisional CO and blocking aids.

GAUGE

18 sts and 36 rows = 4" [10 cm] in garter stitch on US 6 [4 mm] needles and MC. *Before you measure, please take the time to wash and block your swatch in the same manner that you will wash and block your shawl.*

FINISHED MEASUREMENTS

92" [234 cm]

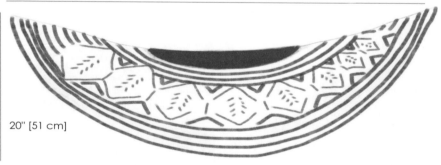

20" [51 cm]

DUST AND CLAY

INSTRUCTIONS

I-CORD CAST ON

Using circular needles and MC, CO 4 stitches using a provisional CO. Do not join.

I-cord setup row (RS): Knit the stitches and slide or slip them back onto the left tip of the needle.

Repeat **Row 1** – 7 times more [8 rows of i-cord worked]. Slide the stitches back onto the left tip, knit 4 sts, pick up and knit 6 stitches from the vertical edge of your i-cord Keep MC attached. Release the provisional CO sts on the needle.

You should have 14 stitches on needle, 4 sts on each end for i-cord finishing and 6 sts picked up from length of the i-cord.

SINGLE COLOUR BEGINNING

Setup Row (WS, MC): Slip the first 4 sts wyif, k1fb, knit to last 5 sts, k1fb, slip the last 4 sts wyif.

Row 1 (RS, MC): K4, slide the 4 sts back onto left needle and k4 again, k1fbf, knit to last 5 sts, k1fbf, k4, slide the 4 sts back onto left needle and k4 again.

Row 2 (WS, MC): Slip the first 4 sts wyif, k1fb, knit to last 5 sts, k1fb, slip the last 4 sts wyif.

Repeat **Rows 1-2** 18 more times. *You should have 130 sts on needle.*

FIRST STRIPES

Attach CC and keep MC attached. Begin striping as follows.

Row 3 (RS, CC): K4, slide the 4 sts back onto left needle and k4 again, k1fbf, knit to last 5 sts, k1fbf, k4, slide the 4 sts back onto left needle and k4 again.

Row 4 (WS, CC): Slip the first 4 sts wyif, k1fb, knit to last 5 sts, k1fb, slip the last 4 sts wyif.

Row 5 (RS, CC): K4, slide the 4 sts back onto left needle and k4 again, k1fbf, knit to last 5 sts, k1fbf, k4, slide the 4 sts back onto left needle and k4 again.

Row 6 (WS, CC): Slip the first 4 sts wyif, k1fb, knit to last 5 sts, k1fb, slip the last 4 sts wyif.

Row 7 (RS, MC): K4, slide the 4 sts back onto left needle and k4 again, k1fbf, knit to last 5 sts, k1fbf, k4, slide the 4 sts back onto left needle and k4 again.

Row 8 (WS, MC): Slip the first 4 sts wyif, k1fb, knit to last 5 sts, k1fb, slip the last 4 sts wyif.

Repeat **Rows 3-8** 9 more times. *You should have 310 sts on needle.*

SHORT ROW LACE

Cut MC and keep CC attached. Begin short row lace.

Row 9 (RS, CC): K4, slide the 4 sts back onto left needle and k4 again, k1fbf, pm, *k2tog 3 times, [yo, k1] 6 times, k2tog 3 times*; repeat * -* once, W&T.

Row 10 (WS, CC): Knit to last 5 sts, k1fb, slip the last 4 sts wyif.

Row 11 (RS, CC): K4, slide the 4 sts back onto left needle and k4 again, k1fbf, k to marker, sm, *k2tog 3 times, [yo, k1] 6 times, k2tog 3 times*; repeat *-* to previous wrapped st, work once more *-*, W&T.

Row 12 (WS, CC): Knit to last 5 sts, k1fb, slip the last 4 sts wyif.

Repeat **Rows 11-12** 4 more times.

Note: You will be adding one more lace repeat on every repeat of Row 11 after the previous turning point. There's no need to pick up the wraps as they will blend in garter st nicely. After the 4 repeats you should have 19 sts between the i-cord and the marker and you can add another repeat of the lace before the marker.

Row 13 (RS, CC): K4, slide the 4 sts back onto left needle and k4 again, k1fbf, pm, *k2tog 3 times, [yo, k1] 6 times, k2tog 3 times*; remove the previous marker, repeat *-* to previous wrapped st, work once more *-*, W&T.

Row 14 (WS, CC): Knit to last 5 sts, k1fb, slip the last 4 sts wyif.

Row 15 (RS, CC): K4, slide the 4 sts back onto left needle and k4 again, k1fbf, k to marker, sm, *k2tog 3 times, [yo, k1] 6 times, k2tog 3 times*; repeat *-* to previous wrapped st, work once more *-*, W&T.

Row 16 (WS, CC): Knit to last 5 sts, k1fb, slip the last 4 sts wyif.

Repeat **Rows 15-16** 4 more times. After the 4 repeats you should have 19 sts between the i-cord and the marker and you can add another repeat of the lace. Then work once more **Rows 13-16** and repeat **Rows 15-16** once.

You should have 355 sts on needle.

SECOND STRIPES

Attach MC and keep CC attached. Begin striping as follows.

Row 17 (RS, MC): K4, slide the 4 sts back onto left needle and k4 again, k1fbf, knit to last 5 sts, k1fbf, k4, slide the 4 sts back onto left needle and k4 again.

Row 18 (WS, MC): Slip the first 4 sts wyif, k1fb, knit to last 5 sts, k1fb, slip the last 4 sts wyif.

Row 19 (RS, CC): K4, slide the 4 sts back onto left needle and k4 again, k1fbf, knit to last 5 sts, k1fbf, k4, slide the 4 sts back onto left needle and k4 again.

Row 20 (WS, CC): Slip the first 4 sts wyif, k1fb, knit to last 5 sts, k1fb, slip the last 4 sts wyif.

Row 21 (RS, CC): K4, slide the 4 sts back onto left needle and k4 again, k1fbf, knit to last 5 sts, k1fbf, k4, slide the 4 sts back onto left needle and k4 again.

Row 22 (WS, CC): Slip the first 4 sts wyif, k1fb, knit to last 5 sts, k1fb, slip the last 4 sts wyif.

Repeat **Rows 17-22** 4 more times. *You should have 445 sts on needle.*

FINAL GARTER STITCH EDGE

Cut CC and continue with MC only. Work **Rows 17-18** 6 more times. *You should have 481 sts on needle.*

BO all on next row using an i-cord BO.

FINISHING

Weave in all yarn ends carefully. Block the shawl to measurements using your preferred method.

GLOSSARY

GLOSSARY OF TERMS AND USEFUL LINKS

Brioche Increase (BrkYObrk)
https://www.purlsoho.com/create/brioche-stitch-basic-increase-bk2tog-yo-bk2tog/

Brioche Decreases (Brk3tog / bsk2p)
https://www.purlsoho.com/create/brioche-stitch-basic-decreases/

Buttonholes
https://www.youtube.com/watch?v=EY4vBzLo-Xs

Cable Cast-On
www.purlsoho.com/create/cable-cast-on

Elastic Bind-Off
Knit 1 stitch, *knit 1, insert the left hand needle into the 2 sts on the right needle (on top of the right needle), knit the 2 sts together through the back loop (1 st left on the right needle); repeat from * until you have bound off all sts.

I-cord Bind-Off
https://www.andrearangel.com/tutorial-blog/2017/5/25/i-cord-bind-off

Knitted Cast-On
Insert the right needle into the first stitch and knit it, but do NOT slip it off of the left needle. Tilt the right needle to the right and insert the left needle into the loop you've pulled up. You are now in position to complete another knit stitch. Repeat the instructions as many times as indicated for the number of stitches to cast on.
https://www.youtube.com/watch?v=IzVy8fRfOw0

Long-tail Cast-On
www.purlsoho.com/create/2006/09/29/long-tail-cast-on

Make Bobble (MB)
Knit into front, back, front, and back of next st on left needle (3 sts increased). Turn work. P4, turn work. K4, turn work. P4, turn work. K4, *with left needle, lift 2nd st on right needle over first st and off needle; repeat from * twice more (3 sts decreased, original stitch count).

Mattress Stitch
https://www.purlsoho.com/create/mattress-stitch/

Provisional Cast-On
www.youtube.com/watch?v=R3J-sUx_whE

Wrap and Turn
www.purlbee.com/2008/06/18/short-rows

ABBREVIATIONS

approx: Approximately

BO: Bind Off

BOR: Beginning of round

bsk2p: Left leaning brioche decrease. Slip 1 brioche stitch with its paired yarn over knitwise, k2tog (the next purl stitch with the foll knit stitch and its paired yarn over), pass the slipped stitch and its paired yarn over together over and off the right needle

brk1:   Brioche knit one; knit the stitch that was slipped in the previous row together with its yarn over

brp1:   Brioche purl one; purl the stitch that was slipped in the previous row together with its yarn over

brkYObrk: Brioche increase: Brk1, do not drop the stitch from the left needle, yo, brk1 into the same stitch. 2 sts increased

brk3tog: Right leaning brioche decrease. K2tog (the next knit stitch with its paired yarn over and the following purl stitch), slip the resulting stitch back to the left needle. Pass the following stitch (a knit stitch and its paired yarn over) over the first stitch on the left needle and off the left needle, move the resulting stitch back to the right needle

C3B: p1	Sl1 onto CN and hold in back, k3, from CN
C3F:	Sl3 onto CN and hold in front, p1, k3 from CN
C4B: in	Slip 2 onto cable needle and hold back, k2, k2 from CN
C4F: in	Slip 2 onto cable needle and hold front, k2, k2 from CN
C6B: in	Slip 3 onto cable needle and hold back, k3, k3 from CN
C6F: in	Slip 3 onto cable needle and hold front, k3, k3 from CN
CC:	Contrasting Color
CO:	Cast On
dpns:	Double-pointed needles
foll(s):	Follows, following

garter st: Garter stitch; Back and forth: knit on RS and WS; In the round: knit one round; purl one round

k:	Knit
ktbl:	Knit through back loop
k1fb: stitch	Knit into front of the stitch, leave on left needle and knit into back of the same stitch; increase
k1fbf: stitch	Knit into front of the stitch, leave on left needle, knit into back of the same stitch and knit again into front of the same stitch; 2 sts increased
k2tog:	Knit 2 sts together; decrease
k3tog:	Knit 3 sts together; 2 sts decreased
m:	Marker
MB:	Make Bobble
MC:	Main Color
m1p: tip,	Purled increase. With left needle

lift strand between needles, from back to front. Purl lifted loop

m1L (purl):	Left slanting increase, make one left; pick up the strand between the stitches from front, purl through the back of the stitch
m1R (purl):	Right slanting increase, make one right; pick up the strand between the stitches from back, purl through the front of the stitch
m1L:	Increase slanted to the left (pick up the horizontal bar between the sts from front to back, knit through back leg)
m1R:	Increase slanted to the right (pick up the horizontal bar between the sts from back to front, knit through front leg)
patt:	Pattern
pm:	Place marker
p:	Purl
p2tog:	Purl 2 sts together; decrease
p3tog:	Purl 3 sts together; 2 sts decreased
pwise:	Purlwise
RS:	Right side

rev St st: Reverse Stockinette stitch; knit on WS, purl on RS

s2kp: over	Slip 2 as if to k2tog, pass slipped sts
sl:	Slip

sl1yo: Slip the next stitch purlwise, then bring the yarn over the needle (and over the slipped stitch) to the back. *Note: working yarn must always be in front before slipping the stitch.*

sm:	Slip marker
ssk: crease	Slip, slip, knit slipped sts tbl; de-
st(s):	Stitch (stitches)
St st:	Stockinette stitch; knit on RS, purl on WS
tbl:	Through back loop
tog:	Together
WS:	Wrong side
wyib:	With yarn in back
wyif:	With yarn in front
W&T: stated	Wrap and turn; work to place in pattern, bring yarn front, slip the next st without knitting it, bring the yarn back, slide the slipped st back on left needle, and turn work
yo:	Yarn over

THANK
YOU

Aimée	*Jonna*
Akshata	*Julie*
Caroline	*Kim*
Cathrin	*Liinu*
Charly	*Maria*
Dianne	*Virginia*
Heather	
Iisakki	
Iris	

*And all our testers.
None of this would be possible
without you!*